W9-CRS-850

KEYS TO RETIREMENT PLANNING

Second Edition

KEYS TO RETIREMENT PLANNING

Second Edition

Warren Boroson

Specialist Editor
The Record
Hackensack, NJ

BARRON'S

© Copyright 1995 by Barron's Educational Series, Inc.
Prior edition © Copyright 1990 by Barron's Educational Series, Inc.

All rights reserved.
No part of this book may be reproduced in any form,
by photostat, microfilm, xerography, or any other
means, or incorporated into any information retrieval
system, electronic or mechanical, without the written
permission of the copyright owner.

All inquiries should be addressed to:
Barron's Educational Series, Inc.
250 Wireless Boulevard
Hauppauge, NY 11788

Library of Congress Catalog Card Number 94-44567

International Standard Book Number 0-8120-9013-6

Library of Congress Cataloging-in-Publication Data
Boroson, Warren.
    Keys to retirement planning / Warren Boroson. — 2nd ed.
        p.   cm — (Barron's business keys)
    Includes index.
    ISBN 0-8120-9013-6
    1. Finance, Personal. 2. Retirement income. I. Title.
II. Series.
    HG179.B5845   1995
    332.024'01—dc20   94-44567
                                                        CIP

PRINTED IN THE UNITED STATES OF AMERICA

5678   5500   987654321

CONTENTS

INTRODUCTION

It's bad enough that most American workers aren't saving enough for their retirement—the little that they do invest, they tend to invest unwisely. And in the future, the situation promises to get worse, not better.

The lessons are: Save earlier, save more, and save more intelligently.

Problem No. 1. The average American, U.S. Government studies show, saves only about 4% of his or her after-tax income. The conventional recommendation: at least 10%, depending on your age.

A survey of preretirees, sponsored by Oppenheimer-Funds and *Money Magazine,* found that "most Americans will probably have only between one-third and one-half the annual income that they will need to retire comfortably," to quote the report.

Some people may think that they are saving via their homes, by making regular mortgage payments and through regular appreciation. There's some truth to this—at least the first part. But houses are no longer the great big piggy bank they once were, and in the next decade they will probably not prove as valuable as they did in the early eighties, when they enjoyed double-digit appreciation.

Yet the OppenheimerFunds/*Money* poll found that 70% of preretirees and 84% of the retirees thought that buying a home is "one of the best ways for a young person to save for retirement."

Preretirees also seem to have the mistaken notion that they will need less to live on than they will really need. Some 60% of the preretirees polled believed that they will be able to live comfortably on less than 60% of their pre-retirement income. But only one-third of retirees themselves were actually living on less than 60% of their annual preretirement polled believed that they will be able to live comfortably on less than 60% of their preretirement income. But only one-third of retirees themselves were actually living on less than 60% of their annual preretirement incomes. The rest needed more to live on.

Problem No. 2. Another mistake people make is investing too conservatively, which generally means not putting enough money into the stock market. Over the years, the stock market has blessed investors with far higher returns than bonds and cash equivalents (like money market funds and short-term certificates of deposit).

Too many investors put too much of their retirement money into such relatively low-paying investments as guaranteed investment contract, certificates of deposit, and money market funds.

The OppenheimerFunds/*Money* poll found that nearly half of the preretirees mistakenly thought that bonds frequently outperformed stocks over long periods of time. Some 16% could not even venture a guess as to which did better.

"Stocks continue to be viewed as volatile, risky investment," the poll found. "Consider that almost half (48%) of the preretirees said that most stock market investors get 'wiped out' at least once in their lifetimes."

Jon S. Fossel, chairman of Oppenheimer, has lamented that "individuals have historically avoided stocks and, to a lesser extent, bonds because of the perception that they are too risky. The irony is that the greatest risk to a secure retirement may be a reliance on low-return, fixed-income investments to fund it.

"When you forgo stocks in your retirement programs, you forgo what historically has been the single best-performing asset class over time," he went on. "Trying to build a winning retirement without equities is like trying to win a football game without passing the ball."

Still, if an investor panics and sells at his or her first exposure to the stock market's volatility, he or she should be warned to stay away from stocks (at least for now). Some investors do panic easily, and it's far better for someone to invest in guaranteed investment contracts than to buy stocks high and sell them low.

Joseph J. Seymour, director of retirement services for Quest for Value in New York City, agrees that some people are too nervous to invest in stocks. "They need to be educated," he argues. "And some will never learn to accept the risk that they should."

Another unwise investment—besides low-paying fixed-income instruments—is company stock, if you own too much of it. Studies have shown that you need 15 to 20 different stocks in your portfolio so as not to risk badly underperforming the stock market (as represented by a mirror of the market, the Standard & Poor's 500 Stock Index). This suggests that you should not have more than 7% in any stock. Yet many investors put as much as one-third of their portfolios into their employer's stock. Sometimes their employers encourage them by providing matching funds only if the employees do buy company stock.

The Institute of Management and Administration in New York City reports that company stock and guaranteed investment contracts constitute more than two-thirds of employee assets at large companies. GICs made up 34.1% of all portfolios, and company stock made up 33.9%. General stocks, the next most popular choice, made up a mere 14.3%.

But "balanced" funds constituted 8.7%, and since balanced funds are usually made up of 60% stocks and 40% bonds, the total that employees at large companies have in stocks could be considered 19.52% (14.3% plus 60% of 8.7%). Bonds made up 4.3% of the portfolios (although GICs are similar to bonds); cash, 3.1%; and "other," 1.6%.

No one is suggesting that you stop buying company stock altogether, or avoid guaranteed insurance contracts altogether, but don't go overboard. Keep the amount you have in company stock no greater than 7%, and force yourself to put as much of your portfolio into the stock market as you can tolerate—if you know you won't have to touch the money for at least five years. (That's how long bear markets—when stocks go down and stay down—tend to last.)

Problem 3. The third worry is that, for a variety of reasons, things are getting worse.

- More and more employees must now invest their own pension money, not leave it to their employers. That's because "defined contribution plans, like 401(k) plans, are supplanting "defined benefit plans," in which employers managed the money. And many employees will make amateurish mistakes in managing their own money—such as investing too conservatively and "shooting where the rabbit was" (buying stocks when they've become overvalued, selling stocks when they've become screaming bargains).
- Preretirees aren't likely to seek out professional advice about investing. In the poll, only 40% of preretirees said that they had ever talked about their retirement savings needs with a professional adviser. That's about the same percentage (39%) who admitted that they had bought a lottery ticket in hopes of funding their retirement.
- Preretirees may live longer than retirees, thanks to advances in health care; therefore they are likelier to outlive their money.

  The U.S. Department of Health and Human Resources reports that today's typical 62-year-old man can expect to live to 83. A typical 62-year-old woman can expect to live to 90. Thus, the time that people spend in retirement can be 20 to 30 years longer than in earlier generations.
- Women in particular may be vulnerable. A nationwide survey by *Executive Female Magazine* found that only 9% of women surveyed felt comfortable making investment decisions. Some 71% of women between 35 and 54 said they did not know how to invest, and 37% of the women in this age group said that they had never made an investment decisions.

  Besides, although more and more women are becoming financially independent, only 50% of women have a current pension plan, reports the National Center for Women and Retirement Research.

All this is especially worrisome considering that the National Center for Women and Retirement Research predicts that, at one time or another, 90% of all women will be entirely responsible for their own financial affairs.

- While talk about Social Security's problems can be exaggerated, the fact is that Social Security benefits are not enough for most people to live on even now. A Social Security Administration report published in 1990 found that only 36% of people's retirement income comes from Social Security.

  Besides, Social Security benefits can now be taxed. And "future tax increases cannot be ruled out," according to a booklet published by the Scudder mutual fund group.

  In addition, by the year 2005 the age for full eligibility for benefits will be 66, not 65. By 2022, it will be 67. And if Social Security's financial underpinnings worsen, the age for eligibility may be raised even higher.

Finally, if you're counting on working to supplement your income during your retirement, be aware that you can lose benefits if you work. For 1994, if you were 65 through 69 and earned more than $11,160, you lost $1 in retirement benefits for every $3 you earned above the limit.

All of which suggests that people had better start saving earlier, saving more, and saving in a more enlightened way, if they are going to spend their retirement years comfortably.

1

NEST EGG

To retire, will you need a $500,000 nest egg? A million? Or a mere $100,000?

There's no one answer. You must consider several factors:

- Your obligations now. Do you still have a house mortgage? Are you sending children through college?
- Your lifestyle. Do you vacation on the Left Bank or just drive to a local beach? Do you head out for a fancy dinner and the theater with your friends every week, or once in a while do you eat at McDonald's and then take in a movie? Do you buy new furniture every few years, or only when what you already own would be rejected by the Salvation Army?
- Where you live—in expensive Honolulu, for example, or in inexpensive Oshkosh.
- Whether you plan to continue working, full-time or part-time.
- Whether you take Social Security payments at 62 or 65—or even later.
- The rate of inflation.
- Your health.

But the fact that there's no single target nest egg for everyone doesn't mean you shouldn't make a ballpark estimate, to check on where you stand now.

Your nest egg will typically consist of your Social Security benefits, pension plans, savings plans, IRAs, investment portfolio, and whatever real estate you own that's convertible into cash. You might take the time now to estimate what you'll receive from them every year in your retirement:

Social Security	_____
Company Pensions	_____
Investments:	
IRAs, Keoghs, SEPs	_____
Annuities	_____
Other	_____
Real Estate	_____
Business Interest	_____

Your house, if you have one, can be a splendid source of money. You can sell it and move into a smaller, less expensive residence.

Homeowners enjoy wonderful tax breaks. Among them: If (a) you're 55 at the time of the sale, (b) it's your main residence, and (c) you've lived there three out of the last five years, you can forget about $125,000 of the capital gains (profit) you've made. Still another tax break: If you buy another main house as expensive as the one you sold, or more expensive, within a two-year period, you can defer paying taxes on your gains. This tactic can be combined with the $125,000 exclusion. If you have a choice, use the tax-deferral strategy: You can always use the $125,000 exclusion later on. Another course is to obtain a "reverse annuity" mortgage, where a lender pays you in exchange for part ownership of your house.

A really tough question is: Should you count on spending some of your nest egg? "Never invade principal" is a cardinal rule of the Old Rich. But if you must, you must. Paul Westbrook of Watchung, NJ, a pension authority and Certified Financial Planner, suggests you go right ahead and crack your nest egg—"Slowly. And cautiously." Other planners recommend that you not invade principal until some years into your retirement, just to be on the conservative side.

In calculating how long your money will last, bear in mind that you may live far longer than you expect. Don't be guided just by the standard longevity tables. To be on the safe side, add ten years to your normal realistic life expectancy. (See Key 3.)

Obviously, if your nest egg yields 8% a year, after taxes, you can withdraw 8% a year without invading principal. But what if you do start spending your nest egg—how long will it last? Check the table below. It shows, for example, that if your money earns 8%, and you spend 10%, your money would last 21 years.

Yield	Years Money Lasts With % of Principal Withdrawn Annually										
	5%	6%	7%	8%	9%	10%	11%	12%	13%	14%	15%
5%	*	37	26	20	16	14	12	11	10	9	8
6%		*	34	24	19	16	13	12	10	9	9
7%			*	31	22	18	15	13	11	10	9
8%				*	29	21	17	14	12	11	10
9%					*	27	20	16	13	12	10
10%						*	26	19	15	13	11
11%							*	24	18	14	12
12%								*	23	17	14
13%									*	22	16
14%										*	21
15%											*

*Indefinitely.
Assumptions: Withdrawals are made each month. Interest is compounded continuously.
Source: U.S. League of Savings Associations

The usual advice is that your nest egg should provide 60% to 70% of your preretirement income. But the higher your preretirement income, the more you can cut back; the less your preretirement income, the less you can cut back. The rich not only get richer; they can afford to get a little poorer. Here's a rough guide:

Annual Income	Needed in Retirement
$30,000	80%
40,000	75%
50,000	75%
60,000	70%
70,000	65%
80,000 or over	60%

At this point, you can figure out roughly what you'll need in retirement. If your gross income is now $50,000, you'll need 75% of that—$37,500. If you count on living another 21 years, and estimate that your nest egg will earn 8% a year (after taxes), and plan on withdrawing 10% a year, you'll need $375,000.

To figure out more precisely what you'll need, consider which of your expenses will be lower, which higher. Your mortgage balance should be low, or perhaps you now own a house outright. You may be in a lower tax bracket. You won't have to commute to work or eat lunches out. Your clothing expenses should decline. You probably won't need as much life insurance, or your premiums may be paid up; if you stop driving to work, your auto insurance premiums may drop; and, if you stop working, you can cancel any disability insurance you're paying on your own. Finally, you won't have to save as much.

But one expense may be greater: health insurance and health care.

Your retirement budget should look something like the figures below.

Housing	33.2%
Food	28.3
Transportation	10.5
Health care	10.7
Clothing	4.0
Entertainment	2.8
Other*	10.5
	100.0

*Personal care, education, charitable contributions, etc.
Source: U.S. Bureau of Labor Statistics

What if you see that you *won't* have enough to retire on—come age 60, 65, or even 70? See the next key for some answers.

2

RIG

The dreaded RIG, or "retirement income gap," is the difference between what you'll have and what you'll need.

Consult some experts, and you may be told you should start saving vast sums every month. Inflation—inexorable, ever-increasing—will supposedly mean that you'll have to be a multimillionaire to be able to retire and afford to eat more than just peanut-butter sandwiches.

Inflation probably *is* unavoidable. But if your investment portfolio is sound, you needn't fret. Your money in cash equivalents (money-market funds, short-term CDs, Treasury bills) will help you almost keep pace. Your stocks should do well enough, at least in periods of moderate inflation. And any hard assets you own—your house in particular—should prosper. *Only if you're heavily into long-term bonds will you suffer.* The solution, obviously, is to keep long-term bonds in your portfolio to a sensible minimum.

From the previous key, you should know how much you will need in retirement and how much you'll have.

Now, figure out your retirement income gap—the difference between the monthly income you'll need, minus the monthly retirement income you'll have available. To help you calculate what you may receive from Social Security, use this table:

Projected Monthly Social Security Benefits
(Maximum at age 65)

Age Now	Worker With Nonemployed Spouse	Worker and Employed Spouse (Both 65)
45	$1,518	$2,024
55	1,393	1,858
60	1,330	1,786

Finally, how to fill the gap: This table, from Franklin Distributors, assumes an (optimistic) 9% fixed-rate of return, compounded monthly, with no fluctuation of principal.

Monthly RIG:	$500	$1,000	$2,000	$3,500	$5,000
Years to invest	You would have to invest these monthly amounts now				
25	$ 43.87	$ 87.94	$ 175.88	$ 307.80	$ 430.71
20	73.01	147.62	295.24	516.87	730.10
10	254.75	509.49	1,018.98	1,783.21	2,547.46

For example, if you're 55 and plan to retire at 65, and your annual retirement income gap is $12,000 a year, you should start saving about $6,114 a year.

If your own RIG seems intimidatingly high, you could cut back on some of your expenses. Spend less on vacations. Don't replace your car, or your furniture, so often. Eat out less.

But there's a less painful alternative: *Become more knowledgeable about investing.* You'll be much further along the way toward filling any RIG you have if you invest your money shrewdly. If you tend to buy this and that stock on a tip, and have no idea what percentage of your assets are invested where, it's unlikely that your savings will grow as much as the savings of someone who has both an overall investment goal and a specific strategy to achieve that goal—and doesn't buy stocks on tips.

To determine which category you fall into, ask yourself: What percentage of your assets are invested in stocks, in bonds, in cash-equivalents, in real estate? How did your investments fare over the last year, the last three years, the last five years? How did they fare compared with the performance of stocks, bonds, and real estate in general? If you don't know the answers, either learn them (the remainder of this book will help), or think about taking less luxurious vacations for a few years.

3

LONGEVITY

When the father of Joseph A. Mintz died in 1954, his mother, 61, inherited $100,000. She thought it was a fortune. Her son, an insurance expert in Dallas, urged her to purchase a single-life annuity, so she would never run out of money, whatever her age. She decided against it.

By age 81, she had gone through the $100,000.

From then on, she lived on meager Social Security payments and family handouts—until she died in 1989, at age 96.

In figuring out how much of a nest egg you'll need for retirement, you must consider your estimated lifespan. On the following page is a table of average life expectancies for people from ages 50 to 84. But because you may live far longer than you expect, add ten years to your own number. Or purchase annuities—which will provide you with regular payments as long as you live, even if you have a family tendency toward Methuselahism.

Expected Additional Years*

Age	Male	Female	Age	Male	Female
30	43.7	49.7	60	18.0	22.5
31	42.7	48.8	61	17.3	21.7
32	41.8	47.8	62	16.7	20.9
33	40.9	46.8	63	16.0	20.1
34	40.0	45.9	64	15.3	19.4
35	39.1	44.9	65	14.7	18.6
36	38.2	44.0	66	14.1	17.9
37	37.3	43.0	67	13.4	17.1
38	36.4	42.1	68	12.8	16.4
39	35.5	41.1	69	12.2	15.7
40	34.5	40.2	70	11.7	15.0
41	33.6	39.2	71	11.1	14.3
42	32.8	38.3	72	10.6	13.7
43	31.9	37.3	73	10.1	13.0
44	31.0	36.4	74	9.6	12.4
45	30.1	35.5	75	9.1	11.7
46	29.2	34.6	76	8.6	11.1
47	28.4	33.7	77	8.2	10.5
48	27.5	32.8	78	7.7	9.9
49	26.6	31.8	79	7.3	9.4
50	25.8	31.0	80	6.9	8.8
51	25.0	30.1	81	6.5	8.3
52	24.1	29.2	82	6.1	7.8
53	23.3	28.3	83	5.8	7.3
54	22.5	27.5	84	5.5	6.8
55	21.8	26.6	85	5.2	6.4
56	21.0	25.8			
57	20.2	24.9			
58	19.5	24.1			
59	18.8	23.3			

*1986 Life Expectancy Table. Department of Health and Human Services, 1990.

4

INVESTMENTS

You could keep your money in a safe-deposit box or hidden behind the baseboard in your closet. But then your money would become less and less valuable as inflation continues. Meanwhile, it wouldn't be earning anything.

The other course is to invest your money.

To play it safe, you could *lend* out your money. The money you lend is your *principal.* The interest you receive is your *yield.* After a specified period of time—3 months, 30 years, whatever—you get your principal back. Such investments are typically called *bonds.* But "fixed-income investments" would be better, because this category includes certificates of deposit, mortgage securities, and other interest-paying investments usually not considered "bonds."

Bonds can offer stability, a regular income, and safety—especially if you keep the terms fairly short and lend money only to prosperous, stable companies. But you probably won't get rich buying bonds. And if inflation comes galumphing back, your bonds will really take a beating. (When interest rates rise, the value of existing bonds falls.)

Ratings of Bonds

	Standard & Poor's	Moody's
Top quality	AAA	Aaa
	AA	Aa
	A	A
Medium quality	BBB	Baa 1-2-3
Speculative	BB	Ba
	B	B
Poor quality	CCC	Caa
	CC	Ca
	C	C

Questionable value	DDD
	DD
	D

One of the ways you can bring some degree of safety and stability to your bond investments is to put your money into top-quality securities. Check the ratings published by Moody's and/or Standard & Poor's.

Another option is to use your money to become an owner, not just a lender. You could become one of the owners of a corporation by buying its stock. Or you could buy into a mutual fund of stocks.

As an owner, you may be fortunate and enjoy enormous profits. If you buy a $1,000 bond, you'll probably get $1,000 back eventually, plus interest. But you might buy a stock for $1,000 and sell it for $10,000. Then again, if you're unlucky, you might wind up asking your broker to take the stock off your hands for $1, just so you can establish a tax loss.

Stocks also tend to be more volatile than bonds, their prices bobbing way up and down. And their yields are almost always less than what you receive from bonds. But unlike bonds, stocks usually do nicely in periods of moderate inflation.

Keep in mind that these are only generalizations. You can buy a bond that pays a whopping 18% interest—but there's a good chance that the company issuing the bond will go into bankruptcy and you'll get very little of your investment back. You can also buy the stock of an electrical utility and get 8% interest, along with very little volatility.

Another broad category of investment is known as "cash" or "cash equivalents." These are short-term debt obligations—money-market funds, certificates of deposit with maturities of a year or less, Treasury bills (with maturities of up to a year). Like bonds, cash equivalents give you a modest return. But the return will help you keep up with inflation, simply because these investments are so temporary. And you'll also enjoy little volatility and plenty of safety.

A final category of investment: hard assets, like real estate, gold, antiques, collectibles. Such investments tend to thrive in inflationary times. Real estate is probably the best of the bunch, and well chosen properties tend to outpace inflation. Debt-free real estate is an especially good investment for older people. Gold and precious metals, by contrast, are extraordinarily volatile.

These four categories aren't mutually exclusive. You can buy the stocks of real estate companies or of companies that mine for gold. And there are investments that don't fit into any of these categories, like options—the right to buy or sell stocks or stock indexes at certain prices. These are highly speculative.

Which investment is best? It depends on your needs and your goals. If you must have regular income to live on, bonds would be better. If you're young and have many years for your investments to flourish, stocks would be the place to be.

If you look at the record, the best investments are stocks and real estate. Bonds, especially long-term bonds, have fared poorly over the years, barely beating the rate of inflation. Gold, for all its volatility, has also barely kept up with inflation.

This doesn't mean that, in the future, stocks will inevitably do better than bonds or gold. But that's the way it has been in the past. And while history isn't destiny, history shouldn't be ignored altogether. As someone has put it, "History doesn't repeat itself, but it does rhyme."

Comparing Investments

Asset	Average Yearly Return
Small-company stocks	12.36%
Common stocks	10.38
Long-term government bonds	5.02
U.S. Treasury bills	3.69
Inflation	3.13

Source: Ibbotson Associates, 1926–1993 returns.

5

MISTAKES

Among the most common investment mistakes of people saving for their retirement—as well as almost everyone else—are the following:

Gambling. The difference between gambling and investing is that, when you invest, you have a far better chance of making a profit. But the pleasures of investing—the excitement, the thrills—are close to those of gambling. And when you find that you're enjoying "investing" so much that you aren't all that concerned about profits, it's time to recognize that you're *gambling.* Other symptoms: You prefer volatile stocks to conservative stocks and mutual funds. You aren't satisfied with small profits.

Playing the sucker. Never buy anything from someone you know only via the telephone. And be wary of prizes you win in contests you did not enter.

Not seeking advice. Many financial advisers are incompetent; many are venal. But this is no excuse for you to yield to the temptation of making decisions entirely on your own. The way to avoid incompetent, venal advisers is to devote your time to finding a competent, conscientious adviser.

Relying too much on others. According to the cliché, "No one cares as much about your money as you do." Actually, salespeople care a whole lot about your money. But certainly no one else will suffer as much as you if your assets begin to shrink. So don't give anyone carte blanche to invest a large percentage of your assets without thoroughly investigating that person.

Not being suspicious enough. Nobody likes suspicious people, always asking rude, insolent questions. But ask yourself: Would you rather be a suspicious person—or a poor person? Bear in mind that there are people out there who will say and do almost anything to separate you from your money. One way to identify these wicked people: You like them a lot. They're charming, friendly, and warm. One good way to protect yourself is to ask another adviser to review any investment proposal.

Not inquiring about commissions. The higher the commission you pay, usually the worse the investment. (See Key 11.)

Making quick decisions. Anytime someone tells you that an investment opportunity is so good that you don't have time to dawdle, *don't* dawdle: Dismiss it out of hand.

Buying high and selling low. Or buying low and selling still lower. This trap is so easy to fall into that even sophisticated investors are seduced. The trouble is that we extrapolate; we figure that whatever has been happening will continue to happen. If a stock has been going up, it will continue going up; if it has been going down, it will continue going down. So we buy an investment when it's climbing—and high-priced. And we sell an investment when it's falling—and low-priced.

Not being humble. Sure, you're smart, resourceful, a quick study. But making money in the market requires the proper personality, not just a high I.Q. You must be willing to admit that you've been positively stupid, and to cut your losses. You must develop the attitude that the right time to buy is often just when almost everyone feels that only an idiot would buy, and the right time to sell is often just when almost everyone feels that only an idiot would sell. You must realize that while the stock market is not totally unpredictable, it's unpredictable enough for you to almost never make really big bets.

Not assessing the risks.

Not paying enough attention to taxes.

Paying too much attention to taxes.

Not monitoring your holdings. Making an investment and putting it into a drawer is almost the equivalent of putting it into the garbage can.

Buying unusual investments. If you can't understand it, forget it. Stick to meat and potatoes—stocks, bonds (CDs,

Treasuries, municipals, corporate bonds), cash, and real estate. Forget about residuals of collaterized mortgage obligations, derivatives, and such.

Being too aggressive. A sign: Your investment portfolio consists almost entirely of stocks, with virtually no CDs and Treasuries.

Being too conservative. A sign: Your investment portfolio consists almost entirely of CDs and Treasuries, with virtually no stocks.

Not checking an investment's yield, if you need income.

Not having a diversified portfolio. (See Key 6.)

Not properly structuring your portfolio. Your investments should be appropriate for a person of your age, your resources, and your financial sophistication. (See Key 27.)

When all is said and done, most older people should invest their retirement money in only one of two ways: conservatively and very conservatively.

6

DIVERSIFICATION

If, on September 30, 1969, you had bought $10,000 worth of Philip Morris stock, around 20 years later, on December 31, 1988, your shares would have been worth $514,700. Congratulations.

If, on September 30, 1969, you had bought $10,000 worth of International Harvester stock, around 20 years later (December 31, 1988), your shares (of Navistar International now) would have been worth $4,113. Rotten luck.

Of course, if you had split your $10,000 between those two stocks, you would have wound up with $259,406.50. Not bad.

The benefits of diversification should be obvious—but they aren't. A man retiring from the Ford Motor Company has his entire pension invested in Ford stock, and he wants to keep all of it there. He asked me, "Isn't Ford a good stock? Isn't it a well-managed company?" Yes and yes. And the gentleman should sell some immediately, then gradually sell a lot more. He may have 30 years to spend in retirement, and during those 30 years Ford may *not* be a good stock and Ford may *not* be a well-run company—and the stock market may not be the place for all his pension money.

Investors must diversify just in case they're wrong, and they've bet on International Harvester and not Philip Morris. Even Michael Price, who runs the Mutual Series Funds in Short Hills, NJ, makes mistakes. But his funds own 200 stocks. A few mistakes on Mike's part won't matter that much as long as he continues picking a great many winners.

You should diversify both *vertically* and *horizontally*.

Vertically means spreading your bets across different stocks in different industries (like Merck in health care, Southwestern Bell in telephones), small company stocks, and foreign stocks. Studies have shown that, to be properly diversified, you should have at least 15 stocks in different industries.

Horizontal diversification means spreading your money across different types of investments. Not just stocks, but cash equivalents, bonds, and real estate. If you're buying stock mutual funds, diversify further by choosing fund managers with different investment strategies—one who invests in stocks of companies with growing earnings, and another who invests in undervalued stocks. While you're at it, diversify your bonds as well, varying them by their maturities (short-term and medium-term) and by their creditworthiness (high-grade bonds, perhaps along with some high-yield or junk bonds). And diversify the *prices you* pay—by investing at regular intervals, not all at once.

Diversification *doesn't* mean buying a little of absolutely everything—from Swiss francs to Chinese ceramics, from pork bellies to puts. Concentrate on the meat and potatoes and skip the petits fours. Cash equivalents, stocks, bonds, and real estate will do, though you might want foreign stocks and bonds, too. Your aim is to spread your bets in such a way that if few of your stocks sink into the pit, some of your other stocks will probably offset your losses by soaring to the heavens. And if the stock market itself plummets, your other investments— cash equivalents, bonds, real estate—may help prop up your sagging portfolio.

For suggestions on how to diversify a portfolio, see Key 27. For suggestions on particular portfolios, see Key 28.

7

RISK

Risk generally means the possibility that you will lose part or all of your original investment. The worst risk— Category 1—is that somebody might abscond with your retirement money, or that a company you invested in may go bankrupt, or that your bonds may go into default.

There are other risks. You might eventually receive all of your original investment back, but the return on your money may be small—lower than the inflation rate. And that means the purchasing power of your original investment has shrunk, too. This is Category 2 risk—not so bad as Category 1, but bad.

Category 3 is the trickiest: the risk of volatility. Let's say that you invest $10,000 in a stock mutual fund. After a year, all you have left is $9,000. But two years after that, you have $12,000.

Is a volatile investment risky? Of course. You may have sold out after year one, either because you needed the money or because you couldn't imagine that your $9,000 wouldn't shrivel further—and that it would climb to $12,000. But volatile investments are not *quite* as risky as Category 1 investments.

Category 3 risks are the only ones we can easily measure—because we can measure volatility. We can, for example, compare an investment's volatility with the ups and downs of a model of the stock market, the Standard & Poor's 500. The S&P 500 is given a "beta" of 1. A stock that's less volatile would have a beta less than 1; a stock that's more volatile would have a beta over 1.

Another way of measuring volatility is not to compare an investment with the S&P 500 but with itself. How much has it bobbed up and down over a period of time? This measure is called the standard deviation, and it's usually more reliable than the beta. You can learn the betas of stocks from Standard & Poor's *Stock Guide,* the betas and standard deviations of mutual funds from *Morningstar Mutual Funds.*

Let's say that you want to buy shares of a stable mutual fund. The standard deviation of the Standard & Poor's 500 (as represented by Vanguard Index Trust-500) was recently 10.09 over a three-year period. The standard deviation of a very stable fund, Lindner Dividend, was 4.62. The standard deviation of a very volatile fund, PBHG Growth, was 23.09. Vanguard Index's annualized 5-year return was 8.94%, Lindner Dividend's, 10.47%; PBHG's was 19.80%. Clearly, Lindner Dividend is impressive both for its stability and its performance.

But the standard deviation is not an unfailing guide to what to buy. PBHG is a splendid fund, despite its volatility. Fairmont, another fund with a high standard deviation (15.51), had an annualized return of only 8.17% over that period. And a fund with low volatility, Beacon Hill Mutual (10.38), had an annualized return of only 8.89%. In short, volatile investments can be good or bad. All you know about a volatile investment is that it's likely to be volatile in the future—and that, if it's like PBHG, it may be rewarding despite its volatility, assuming that you have the time and the courage to wait out declines.

You could, if you wish, avoid all risks. Money market funds, certificates of deposit, and Treasury bills are virtually riskless. You're almost certain to get back whatever money you put in, and the interest you earn should be a bit ahead of the inflation rate. (A small money market fund in Colorado did lose money in 1994.)

The trouble is, the interest you receive probably won't be *much* ahead of the inflation rate. To make more money, you must assume more risk with at least a portion of your portfolio.

The conventional wisdom is that the more risk, the more reward. But it's not true. Blue-chip stocks are fairly safe, yet they have proved unusually rewarding. Commodities are unusually risky, and as investments they have stunk to high heaven.

Here's how investments are usually rated as to their general riskiness, from very risky to very safe:

Highest risk	Commodities
	Collectibles
	Precious metals
	Purchase of options
	Very small-company stocks
	Oil and gas exploration
	Raw land
	Small-company stocks & mutual funds
	Low-grade bonds
	Long-term bonds
	Investment real estate
	Blue-chip stocks & mutual funds
	Stock-and-bond mutual funds
	High-grade bonds, short/intermediate term
	Fixed annuities/ insurance contracts
	Personal residential real estate
	Money market funds
	Savings accounts
Lowest risk	Savings bonds
	Certificates of deposit
	Treasury bills

These rankings are rough: Much depends on the specific investment. Low-grade bonds, for example, can differ very much from one another, as can small company stocks.

But most investors nearing retirement should concentrate on investments in the last two categories—and skip over investments in the top two.

8

INFLATION

If you're as old as the author, you can recall when $12,000 a year was considered a lordly income, when the only houses that sold for $100,000 were mansions, and when pennies actually *bought* something.

Inflation is still hanging around. And for the retirement-minded, who are typically dependent on fixed income investments, it's Public Enemy No. 1.

If inflation were to continue at only 5% a year, prices would double in 14.4 years. That would mean that a $300,000 nest egg would be worth only $150,000. And bear in mind that if you're a male and 65, your life expectancy is 14.4 years. If you're a woman of 70, your life expectancy is 15.2 years.

If the past is any guide, one of the best ways to keep your assets growing above the rate of what we now consider "moderate" inflation is to own stocks. For maximum safety, invest in a replica of the stock market itself—a mutual fund like Vanguard Index Trust-500. Real estate is also safe.

In times of *rapid* inflation, however, stocks haven't always been the best sanctuary. Hard assets—real estate, gold, silver—have fared much better. In recent years, short-term debt has also been a safe refuge.

Annual Rates of Return During Moderate Inflation

	CPI	Stocks	Bonds	Short-term Debt	Housing	Gold
1899–1915	1.3%	8.2%	4.1%	5.3%	5.7%	—
1942–1945	2.5	26.1	4.5	0.9	10.0	—
1951–1965	1.6	16.5	2.2	3.5	5.5	—
Average	1.4	13.8	3.8	3.7	7.1	—
1982–1987	3.5	17.3	16.0	8.0	5.5	3.4

Source: Morgan Stanley Research. CPI = Consumer Price Index, a measure of inflation. Short-term debt = Treasury bills and commercial paper.

In times of *deflation,* when prices fall, stocks, housing, and precious metals generally perform disgracefully, but bonds and short-term debt come into their own. (Interest rates fall, making existing bonds more valuable.)

But remember that history offers only clues. We're not dealing with the immutable laws of physics or chemistry. Particular circumstances can change—and these general guidelines might not obtain. If stocks are overvalued at the beginning of a period of moderate inflation, they may fare poorly. If the world is awash with gold at the start of a period of rapid inflation, its price may not rise as it has in the past.

Annual Rates of Return During Rapid Inflation

	CPI	Stocks	Bonds	Short-term Debt	Housing	Gold
1914-1919	13.3%	11.6%	2.1%	4.7%	17.5%	—
1949-1947	6.8	12.3	2.6	1.0	12.2	—
1949-1951	5.8	24.8	0.9	2.3	10.2	—
1965-1971	4.0	6.4	6.1	6.8	10.3	31.6%
1971-1981	8.3	5.8	3.8	8.8	10.3	28.0
Average	8.3	12.2	3.1	4.7	12.1	11.9

Source: Morgan Stanley Research

These are among the best arguments for diversifying your assets—and keeping the maturities of your bonds short, or varied.

9

SAVING WHEN YOU'RE YOUNG

Young people really shouldn't be expected to make saving for their retirement their chief investment goal. They may have many other reasonable goals: saving to get married, to start a family, and to buy a house, or to start their own business, or to take courses to improve their job skills, or saving to send their own children through college . . . even to have enjoyable vacations, to buy newer cars, or to travel around the world.

In my own youth, I didn't save for my retirement; the time I spent thinking about finances was devoted to determining which bills I could pay and which I might safely ignore.

It's true that the earlier you start to save for your retirement, the better. The mathematical advantage of saving something while you're in your twenties is astonishing.

Note well: If a 19-year-old puts away $2,000 into an IRA, and continues doing so until age 26, and stops, he or she will have $1,035,160 at age 65 (assuming that the money earns 10% a year).

On the other hand, if a 27-year-old starts putting $2,000 a year into an IRA, and continues putting in $2,000 a year until age 65, he or she will have only $883,185—significantly less.

Even so, when I started an IRA for my 18-year-old son after he earned some money at a summer job, then explained to him that he could withdraw the money without penalty only when he was 59½, he began wondering about my sanity.

It's also true that, in the years to come, Social Security is not likely to be the life preserver it was in the past.

Because of the decline in the number of current workers (the result of the "birth dearth"), benefits may eventually have to be curtailed or postponed, or both.

Still, no one really wants to first become wealthy at the age of 60—and only then begin enjoying life without having stopped to smell the flowers along the way.

Nonetheless, there are good reasons for young people to think of contributing something to a retirement plan where they work, and even to put money into a deductible IRA (if they qualify) or (if they're self-employed) a Keogh (HR-10) or Simplified Employee Pension. First, they will get accustomed to investing, and learn from the experience. Second, if their employer contributes to their retirement plan at work, they should not resist; unless they participate, they will be throwing away easy money. And in the case of hardship, they can probably withdraw or borrow the money before they reach retirement age. Third, even if they must withdraw the money and pay the 10% tax penalty, thanks to the tax deferral, they may be ahead of the game if they have waited for about 15 years.

Most people start seriously saving for their retirement in their fifties, when their children are on their own. It would certainly be wise to start saving something while only in your forties, and desirable—if you can afford it— to start saving in your thirties.

Where should you invest your retirement savings? The conventional wisdom is: entirely in the stock market, and in small company stocks to boot, because they have outperformed large-company stocks. (In 1987, I put my 18-year-old son's IRA money into the Acorn Fund, which invests in small-company stocks.)

But young people, like the rest of us, may panic and sell their stocks if they do poorly. It is better that a young person start with some conservative investments before trying to swim in the deepest part of the pool. A balanced mutual fund—stocks and bonds—might be a good, conservative first choice. Vanguard Wellington or Fidelity Puritan are examples. Later on, the young person should invest in more adventuresome funds, those that invest in small companies, such as PBHG (1-800-809-8008) and Kaufmann (1-800-237-0132).

What percentage of a young person's portfolio should be in the market? It depends on his or her other goals. If the young person wants to buy a house soon, or wants to go to college or graduate school, that person should not have an unlimited exposure to very volatile stocks, which might be depressed when money is needed.

If the young person does not have other goals, he or she might put as much as 80% of his portfolio in stocks. One reason for the 80% figure: Few people are brave enough to tolerate the volatility of a portfolio more than 80% in the stock market.

A bad mistake is to invest in only one mutual fund; that's putting too many eggs in one basket. When my eldest son was born, I invested $10,000 in a famous stock mutual fund for him. Ten years later, the $10,000 had turned into . . . $10,000! Up to that decade, the fund had enjoyed a marvelous record. So, when that son grew up, after investing in Acorn for his IRA, I helped him to diversify his portfolio into Fidelity, Vanguard, Founders, Gabelli, Lindner, and Neuberger & Berman funds.

10

LIQUIDITY

It's an advantage if an investment is liquid; you can quickly sell out for cash. That means you can promptly get money in an emergency, or you can readily switch investments if you think the time is ripe.

Stocks are supposedly "liquid." You can sell them any time the markets are open. But, as investors in stocks discovered on October 19, 1987, small company stocks can be "thinly traded"—not many shares may be out there. Some brokers who specialized in small-company stocks weren't even answering their phones on that terrible Monday because there were so few buyers.

Whether or not a bond is liquid also depends on how many shares are outstanding. A bond issued by General Motors, and listed in the newspaper tables, is obviously far more liquid than a bond issued by a small company or a small municipality.

Real estate is the supreme example of a nonliquid asset. You cannot quickly turn your house, or a real estate limited partnership, into money in the bank. But real estate investment trusts are different: Because they're stocks, they're as liquid as other stocks.

Liquidity should also mean that the investment's price is stable. Ideally, you want an investment that you can sell anytime without sustaining big losses. Most stocks therefore wouldn't qualify. Blue-chip stocks are an exception: Their trading range is usually narrow.

To determine how volatile particular stocks or stock mutual funds are, check their "betas"—their volatility vis-a-vis the Standard & Poor's 500. The S&P 500's beta is 1. A fund like Mutual Shares, recently had a beta of 0.45, meaning that it was less than half as volatile as the stock market as a whole. A mutual fund that has a low beta may either concentrate on stable stocks or include bonds in its portfolio as well. (The betas of funds that invest in precious metals, or in foreign stocks, can be misleading.)

If you include price stability as a criterion for liquidity, long-term bonds wouldn't qualify, either. Interest-rate changes have made their prices leap up and down. The shorter a bond's maturity, usually the more stable its price is. A major exception: low-rated or junk bonds, which can be as volatile as stocks.

So, if you're looking for true liquidity, stick to popular investments with price stability—like cash equivalents (money market funds and Treasury bills). At a level up, look for short- or intermediate-term, widely traded, investment-grade bonds or Treasuries. Still higher up are widely held stocks of old-line companies, stocks that pay relatively high dividends.

Below are some sample betas for various stable mutual funds.

Low Beta Stock Funds

Fund	Beta
Crabbe Huson Equity	0.69
Franklin Balance Sheet	0.52
Gabelli Asset	0.68
Lindner	0.49
Mutual Shares	0.53

Source: *Morningstar Mutual Funds*, 1994.

11

COMMISSIONS

The riskier the investment, usually the higher the commission you'll pay. That's the conclusion of former stockbroker Mary Calhoun.

Why? An innocent answer is that brokers and financial planners have to spend more time explaining complicated, risky investments (like limited partnerships) to their customers. A more cynical answer is that the extra commission compensates the sales agent for having to work hard to ram the product down the customer's throat—and for any subsequent injury to his or her conscience.

Sometimes commissions are almost unavoidable, as when you buy insurance. But even here, high commissions are associated with terrible products: Old fashioned whole-life insurance paid a little over 3% a year and compensated the insurance agent with up to half the first year's premium.

Sometimes high commissions *aren't* accompanied by high risk. You'll pay a broker 5.75% of your investment to buy shares of mutual funds sold by the American Funds in Los Angeles. You'll pay nothing to buy the shares of mutual funds sold by the Monitrend family in Cresskill, NJ. The American Funds have superb long-term records, while the Monitrend funds have dreadful records. Explanation: Reputable brokers will sell shares of the American Funds.

Still, the point is that high commissions can hurt you in two ways. You'll have less money working for you. And the product itself may be poor.

As a rough rule, too, advisers who are not compensated only by commissions have higher ethical standards—accountants have better reputations than real estate agents and stockbrokers. (This may change now that accountants are permitted to accept commissions for products they sell.)

Two lessons: (1) Try to compensate any adviser by means of fees, not commissions. Given a choice between a fee-only financial planner and another kind of planner, choose the fee-only. And (2) always inquire, before you buy any product, whether you are paying a commission, and if so, how much. Anyone who tries to sell you a product *without* telling you the commission he or she would receive is probably someone you should stop doing business with.

Commissions on a $10,000 Investment

$400–$1,000: Limited partnerships
$300–$1,000: Common stock—initial public offering
$600: New closed-end mutual fund
$400–$850: Load, open-end mutual fund
$400–$600: Options; annuities and life insurance
$300–$490: Unit investment trusts
$200–$250: Stocks on New York Stock Exchange
$50–$100: Municipal or corporate bonds
$50: Treasury securities

Source: *Guide to Investor Protection*, Mary Calhoun.

12

YIELDS

A high yield is like an ice cream sundae—very nice indeed, unless the rest of the meal consisted of bread and water. The entire meal is your "total return": your yield *plus* what happened to your original investment.

The yield, of course, is the income you regularly receive from any investment. It's expressed, mathematically, as the income you receive every year as percentage of your principal.

Let's say that you buy $5,000 worth of a stock trading at $50 a share. You own 100 shares. The stock's dividend is $1 a share every three months. So you receive $100 four times a year, or $400. Divide that by $5,000 to get your annual yield: 8%.

But let's say that the stock's price declines to $40 a share. You now own only $4,000 worth of the stock, and your yield is 10%. Are you overjoyed? Would you like to receive a 12% yield—by having your original investment decline to $33⅓ a share?

The danger, of course, is that you can receive a high yield from an investment, but if the principal keeps shrinking, your total yield will eventually plummet into the pits. For example, Piper Jaffray Institutional Government Income was recently yielding 10.84%. But the fund's total return over the past three years, annualized, was a mere 0.35%—including those terrific yields.

People experienced in buying stocks know that a high yield can be a warning. Stocks with high yields may have fallen upon hard times, and the companies may be preparing to cut or even eliminate their dividends.

But people who have bought only certificates of deposit and money market mutual funds may *not* understand that a high yield can be a warning. The reason is that, with CDs and money market funds, there's no difference between the yield and the total return. If you invest $1,000, you get your $1,000 back.

That's not the case with stocks—or with bonds, if you sell them before they mature, or if you buy them after they've first been issued, above or below their original price. And it's not the case with stock or bond mutual funds. You *won't* receive your original investment back intact. You'll receive more, or less, depending on how the investment has fared. (Exception: with unit investment trusts, a form of bond mutual fund, you should get your original investment back, minus your sales commission.)

Theresa A. Havell, an analyst with Neuberger & Berman in New York, offers excellent advice: "Concentrate on a fund's total return, not the yield."

Another important point is that, with bonds, the most important yield is the *yield to maturity.* Bonds have various types of yields. The *coupon* or *nominal* yield is what the bond paid when first issued. Suppose that in 1986 you bought a new bond issued by Graystark, a fictitious company. Its coupon yield: 13¼%. That means it was paying $132.50 a year—$66.25 every six months on each unit of $1,000 (the *par value, face value,* or *principal*). The bond will mature—come due—in the year 2000. (In the papers, the bond might be listed under New York Stock Exchange Bonds: Graystark 13¼ 00).

Suppose that interest rates in general have climbed, or that the company has gotten into trouble and investors are worried that the company may not be able to repay the debt. If you sold the bond early in 1995 you received only $520 on each unit. (It was selling *at a discount.*) Your current yield: 25.5% ($132.50 divided by $520). If you could have sold the bond for, say, $1,100, for only a 12% current yield, the bond would have been trading *at a premium.*

But, when your $520 Graystark bond matures, you're entitled to $1,000 of principal—for a capital gain of $480, you would receive a yearly 30% *yield to maturity.* (When you first bought the bond, the coupon yield of 13¼% was also the yield to maturity because, at maturity, you were scheduled to receive your original investment back.)

So, if you really want to know what a bond's yield is, concentrate on its yield to maturity.

When you stay with simple investments, such as CDs and NOW accounts, you need only focus on the interest rate and the interest you earn on your interest. This is compound interest, and you should focus on how often the interest is compounded; daily is better than monthly, for example. If the interest you earn isn't compounded, you have *simple* interest. But even simple interest can be better than interest compounded "continuously" if the *effective interest rate* is higher. The effective rate is what you receive, including compounding.

If you're ever in doubt about which savings vehicle pays more, ask the lender, "How much money will I receive at the end of the time period?"

A bank's passbook savings account, by the way, is one of the very lowest-paying investments. Worse, the low yield you receive may be eaten into by fees. You'll usually be better off using a credit union. And while a bank's money market deposit account is better than a passbook account, even that typically yields far less than a money market mutual fund.

13

CERTIFICATES OF DEPOSIT

Dull as ditchwater—but perfect for people who want regular income without risk.

Unlike stocks, bonds, and fixed-income mutual funds, the cash value of CDs won't fluctuate. You'll get your investment back intact if you hold on until the CD comes due. You won't pay commissions to buy or sell, as you must with stocks and bonds. And CDs usually pay more than money market mutual funds.

CDs do have drawbacks. If you withdraw your money before maturity, you may pay a penalty. If you tie up your money for a long time, interest rates may rise, and you'll be sitting there with a low-paying investment. CDs are not a hedge against inflation.

The solution is to stagger your maturities—for example, buy some CDs that come due in six months, some in two years, some in five years.

Check the "effective yield" of any CD—what it's paying, with the compounding (reinvestment) of your interest. The more frequent the compounding, the better. "Simple interest," without compounding, is the worst. A $10,000 one-year CD with an interest rate of 8%, compounded daily, would yield $833. A CD with 8% interest and no compounding ("simple interest") would yield only $800. (The difference between "continuous" and "daily" compounding is tiny.) Of course, 8.4% simple interest is better than 8% compounded daily.

Stick with institutions that are members of the Federal Deposit Insurance Corporation, which insures individual accounts up to $100,000.

Don't be lazy and buy CDs only from your local bank. To find the highest-paying CDs around the country, check financial publications. If the business section of your newspaper doesn't publish a list, check *Barron's,* or the *Wall Street Journal* on Thursdays. Wire your money in and out, so as not to lose a few days' interest.

Many brokerage houses also offer CDs now, often with high yields, and you can cash these in before maturity without penalty—but sometimes for a fee, and for a loss if interest rates have risen. (Always ask: If I invest *x*, what will I receive when the CD matures?) Still, such CDs are federally insured because they come originally from banks.

These days, some banks are offering CDs that allow you to switch to a higher interest rate at one time during the life of the CD. But such CDs start out with lower interest rates. Other banks aren't charging penalties for early withdrawals at certain times.

Some suggestions:

- You may be able to defer taxes on a CD if its maturity is one year or less. You could buy a six-month CD in July 1995, get credit for your interest in January, and not report the interest until April 1996.
- Check to see if you can make further contributions to a CD, at the original interest rate, even if rates have sunk.
- Inquire into "floating-rate" CDs, where the interest rate moves along with the prime rate (what lenders charge their most favored customers).
- Ask about an institution's penalty for early withdrawal. The penalties can range from the loss of three months' interest (the mildest) to "replacement cost" (the stiffest). With a mild penalty, you may be better off paying it and investing in a higher-paying CD. Let's say that you buy a $10,000, five-year CD paying 9%. You would have $15,657 after five years. If interest rates rose to 12% and you withdrew your money at the end of one year, paid the three-months interest penalty, and reinvested at 12% for the next four years, you would wind up with $17,272 after the five years. But with the whopping replacement-cost penalty, you would never be better off paying it and buying a higher-yielding CD.

14

MUTUAL FUNDS

A mutual fund is a bit like an investment club. You and other investors pool your money to buy securities. And because there's so much money in the pot, the fund can buy a wide variety. You can also afford to hire a professional manager to decide which securities to buy, and when to sell them. Thus, a mutual fund gives you *diversification* and *professional management.*

Buying mutual funds sure beats what many other investors do—buy and sell a crazy quilt of stocks and bonds under the guidance of a local stockbroker. You'll usually do better paying investment geniuses like Robert Sanborn (Oakmark), Mario (Gabelli Asset), or Michael Price (Mutual Shares, Qualified, and Beacon) to supervise your investment portfolio.

True, mutual funds can be bewildering. To begin with, there are three basic varieties of funds, and all kinds of subvarieties.

The best-known kind of fund is an *open-end investment company.* You buy and sell shares directly through the fund; the fund continually issues new shares. If you use brokers or financial planners, you usually pay these intermediaries a commission. That commission, or "load," could be 1% up to 8.5% of whatever you invest. Over the years, the load may not amount to much compared to your profits from a stock fund, but for a few years the commission will be a drag. Sophisticated investors generally confine themselves to "no-load" or "low-load" funds.

A second type of fund is a *closed-end investment company.* Closed-ends are like stocks, and usually trade on exchanges; the number of shares is fixed. The price per share depends on what investors will pay to buy them— not necessarily on the underlying value of the funds' securities. Oddly enough, many closed-end funds—especially stock funds—sell at a discount to their underlying worth, or net asset value. But it's no free lunch: You could buy a closed-end at a discount, then eventually sell it at a wider discount.

There's a good rule to follow if you're considering a closed-end fund: *Never buy a new issue.* Almost all new funds fall to a discount after brokers stop pushing them onto their customers. Another good rule: *Buy a closed-end when it's trading at the low end of its trading range.*

Among the most desirable closed-ends are those managed by famous investors like John Neff, Martin Zweig, and Mario Gabelli. Gabelli, who also manages open-end funds, thinks closed-ends are better—if you don't trade them frequently and get eaten alive by commissions—simply because of those discounts.

A closed-end fund has one decided advantage over an open-end: The managers don't have to sell the funds' securities if, in a panic, investors start selling their shares. The managers of open-ends may be forced to toss out desirable stocks at low prices just to pay off investors who get antsy and redeem their shares.

A third main type of mutual fund is a *unit investment trust.* Whereas the managers of open and closed-end funds continually buy and sell securities, the managers of UITs keep their portfolios unchanged. They just buy a bunch of bonds—municipals or corporate—and hang on until the bonds come due, usually in 15 or 20 years. You'll pay a commission to buy a UIT, typically 4.5%, but you won't have high continuing expenses to pay because the managers do so little. Usually you can sell your shares of a UIT to the fund before the maturity date.

The trouble with UITs is that they *are* unmanaged. There's no one at the helm checking whether a particular bond should be cast adrift because the company that issued it is going down the drain. (UITs can replace bonds that go into default, though.) Besides, no one tracks the performances of UITs as a group. And their performances may suffer if a good number of bonds in the trust go into default, or if those with high yields are paid off before maturity—"called." Still, for investors who want a regular income and a diversified basket of bonds, UITs can be a good way to go.

Mutual funds can invest in almost anything—common stocks, preferred stocks, low-rated corporate bonds, high-rated corporate bonds, high rated municipals, low-rated municipals, Treasuries, mortgage backed securities, stocks of a single country, stocks in a single industry (like telecommunications), real estate investment trusts, precious metals, options, convertible bonds, short-term debt instruments.

For older investors, index funds should have special appeal. These are funds that just emulate replicas of markets as a whole, like the Standard & Poor's 500 Stock Index. Index funds tend to do better than the majority of managed funds, whether they're stock or fixed-income funds. They're safe and solid.

Three index funds of special interest, because of their low expenses, are

1. Vanguard Index Trust-500, which tracks the S&P 500
2. Vanguard Index Extended Market, which tracks small-company stocks through the Wilshire 4500
3. Vanguard Bond Index Total Bond, which tracks the Salomon Brothers Broad Investment-Grade Bond Index. Vanguard's phone number: 1-800-662-7447.

Another fund group that older investors might be intrigued by is the asset-allocation funds, which try to offer one-stop portfolios. For more on such funds, see Key 26. For more on stock funds, see Key 24; for fixed-income funds, Key 22; for money market funds, Key 15.

You can track how a fund is doing by checking a daily newspaper. But to determine how a fund has been faring against its peers, or over a long period of time, you need a newsletter. For the serious investor in mutual funds, *Morningstar Mutual Funds* is a good though expensive choice ($395 a year; published every two weeks by Morningstar Inc., 53 West Jackson Blvd., Chicago, IL 60604).

Type of fund	Sold by	Shares redeemable at net asset value?	No. of shares	Managed?*
Open-End	Brokers or through fund	Usually	Varies	Yes
Closed-End	Brokers	No	Stays the same	Yes
Unit Trust	Brokers	Yes	Stays the same	No

*Managed = whether the fund regularly buys and sells its holdings.

15

MONEY MARKET FUNDS

These popular funds are not just super checking accounts. They're a good way to keep your assets appreciating in line with inflation. While you may have repressed the memory, back in the early inflationary 1980s some money market funds were paying almost 18%. And if interest rates ever soar again, you can be sure that the interest paid by money market funds will climb with them.

Money market funds invest in short-term debts—jumbo CDs (those of $100,000 and over), Treasury bills, and commercial paper (corporate debts).

"General purpose" money funds are run by mutual funds; "broker-dealer" money funds are run by brokerage houses; "money market deposit accounts" are run by banks and savings and loans. These last tend to pay the least, and typically limit the number of free checks you can write. But they have the advantage that their deposits are usually federally insured up to $100,000 per account. Still, sophisticated investors usually avoid money market deposit accounts.

Money market mutual funds are *almost* perfectly safe. While even short-term interest rates bob up and down, the managers of the funds vary their *yields*, keeping each fund's price per share fixed (usually at $1). While a money market fund can stretch its loans' average maturities to 90 days, almost all keep the average shorter, stretching and shortening in accordance with the way interest rates seem to be heading. (If a fund lengthens the average maturities of its holdings, the manager thinks interest rates are sinking. If the manager shortens them, he or she thinks interest rates are rising.)

The first time any money market fund got into serious trouble was in 1978, when the manager of a tiny fund extended the average maturity on his loans to 650 days. Interest rates rose; the fund's price per share fell to 93 cents. The fund, First Multifund for Income, liquidated, and investors lost 7% of their principal. (Okay, with a maturity of 650 days, it wasn't *really* a money market fund anymore. But, in 1994, a Colorado fund that used risky derivatives experienced a loss.)

The shorter the average maturity of a fund's loans, the safer. But you might sacrifice some yield with such a fund. A better course may be simply to avoid a fund whose average loans' maturities are much longer than their competitors are. (The weekly listings of money market funds in many newspapers typically give their average maturities.) Another slightly risky way for a fund to boost its yield is to buy Eurodollars (deposits in foreign branches of U.S. banks) or low-grade commercial paper. Still, William E. Donoghue, a foremost authority on money market funds, thinks these dangers are "more theoretical than real."

But don't let anyone tell you different: The spreads between the yields of various money market funds can be *enormous*. Three funds with reliably high yields are Fidelity Spartan (800-544-6666); Dreyfus Worldwide (800-645-6561); and Vanguard Prime (800-662-7447). Before buying into any fund, check its yield against these three heavyweights. Dreyfus offers high yields because it invests heavily in Eurodollars; Spartan, because it charges investors for the checks they write and other transactions, and sets a $20,000 minimum; Vanguard, because it has low expenses. All three mutual fund families are top-drawer, and you can readily switch among their funds if you wish.

If you keep only a few hundred dollars in a fund, go ahead and use a bank's money market deposit account. But if you have $1,000 or more in such an account, consider shopping out of town at a mutual fund. And arrange for the fund to wire money to your bank when you need it; don't use regular mail and forgo a few days' interest on a large amount of money.

You can also invest in money market funds that hold municipal bonds or Treasuries. Municipals issued by your own state may make sense if your state levies high income taxes. A fund made up of Treasuries may make sense if you can't afford the $10,000 minimum for a Treasury bill, you want immediate access to your money, and you're determined to wear stretch pants with a belt and suspenders.

16

U.S. SAVINGS BONDS

While they may seem like the poor person's Treasuries, U.S. savings bonds have an advantage over even Treasuries: You can use them to defer paying taxes on your interest until far in the future—12 years, and more.

As is the case with Treasuries, interest from Series EE bonds is exempt from state and local taxes, and the bonds themselves are as sound an investment as you can buy. They don't pay badly, either: Every six months, their rate is set at 85% of the yield on five-year Treasuries for the previous half-year, or at a 4% yield, whichever is higher.

Like T-bills, savings bonds sell at a discount from their face value. A $50 bond, for example, sells for $25. At maturity, you receive the $50. That makes these bonds especially suitable for someone nearing retirement age. You can invest in the bonds before retiring, then receive the entire accumulated interest when you retire and may be in a lower tax bracket.

Some restrictions: You can't buy Series EE bonds with a face value of more than $30,000 in any calendar year in one person's name. You can't use them as collateral for a loan. You can't cash them in during the first six months. If you do cash them in within five years, your interest rate shrinks.

That's why it's a good idea to buy a variety of savings bonds, not just a few with high face values. With a lot of small bonds, you can cash in a few during an emergency and not wind up with a low interest rate on a big pile of money.

When your Series EE bonds mature, continue holding them, or roll them over into Series HH bonds. Series HH bonds pay current interest, and the rate is fixed. You can buy them only with at least $500 of Series EE or the older Series E bonds. Series HH bonds mature in ten years, but the interest is reportable every year. There's no reduction in the interest rate if you cash them in early.

You can buy U.S. savings bonds from banks, savings and loan associations, Federal Reserve banks, or through your employer's payroll deduction plan, if there is one.

The interest on savings bonds will be tax-free if you use the proceeds to pay for the higher education of your dependents, yourself, or your spouse. You must be 24 or older and must have bought the bonds after December 31, 1989. As of 1994, you begin losing the tax break when your adjusted gross income is between $61,850 and $91,850 (for couples filing jointly) or between $41,200 and $56,200 (for singles). The exclusion is phased out at $91,850 for couples, $56,200 for others.

17

TREASURIES

Your single *safest* investment is Treasury bills—not Treasury notes or bonds, which come due (mature) later than T-bills. But to invest in T-bills, you'll need a minimum of $10,000 (unless you invest in a mutual fund that buys Treasury bills). Treasury bills are sold with three-month, six-month, and 52-week maturities.

All Treasury obligations offer benefits that you may not receive from other types of fixed-income investments:

- There's virtually no credit risk. If the U.S. Government defaulted on its obligations to pay off its Treasuries, it would be twilight in America.
- There's little risk of a Treasury's being called—paid off prematurely, typically when current interest rates have sunk. T-bonds can be called five years before they come due. But no bonds have been called since 1962.
- There's no "event risk"—no one is going to buy out the U.S. Government, lowering the ratings of its debt obligations.
- Interest is exempt from state and local taxes.

Treasury bills mature in up to a year; Treasury notes in two to ten years; Treasury bonds in ten to 30 years. The only risk you face when you buy Treasury notes and bonds is that current interest rates will rise. You may then be stuck with a relatively low-paying investment, and—if you sell—you will receive less than you paid. The way to avoid this, of course, is to concentrate on T-bills, but usually T-bills pay less than notes and bonds. For a higher yield you could mix up your investments, buying both bills and notes. You could stagger their maturities, so that every few years you have obligations coming due that

44

you can reinvest at current, possibly higher rates. Or you could use the "barbell" approach—weighting your portfolio heavily toward short-term and longer-term obligations. (Long-term Treasuries are especially volatile, however, and many investors avoid them altogether—except in zero-coupon form, where you receive all your interest in one lump sum, at maturity.) Another way to diversify your maturities is to buy shares of a mutual fund that invests in bills, notes, and bonds, though you would have to pay yearly management fees.

Besides their sensitivity to interest-rate risk, another drawback of Treasury obligations is that their interest rate is usually lower than the rate on corporate bonds.

T-bills are issued in minimum denominations of $10,000 and multiples of $5,000 beyond that. The Treasury won't buy them before they mature, but you can sell them through a bank or brokerage firm. T-bills don't pay regular interest: Like U.S. savings bonds, they're sold at a discount to their face value. Your return is the difference between what you pay and what you receive shortly after you invest. If one-year T-bills are paying 10%, you will quickly receive $1,000 back from a $10,000 investment, and your original $10,000 a year later. (Thus, the true rate of interest is higher than 10%: The "coupon equivalent" yield here would be 11.11%—$1,000 divided by $9,000.)

You owe federal taxes on a T-bill when it matures or when you sell it, even if you received your discount in the previous year. With proper timing, you can defer your tax bill—buying a six-month T-bill in late July, for example.

You can buy T-bills directly through a branch of the Federal Reserve Bank, or—for a fee of around $50—through a bank or broker. An advantage of buying a T-bill through an intermediary is that it's easier to sell it before maturity. You cannot sell issues you bought directly from the Fed within 20 days of your purchase or within 20 days before maturity.

When you buy any kind of Treasury, you can make either a competitive or noncompetitive bid. Stick with noncompetitive bids—which means you'll pay the average rate at the auction. Otherwise, you may pay too much, or—if you've offered too little—you'll risk having your bid rejected.

For more information on buying T-bills and other Treasuries, write to the Bureau of the Public Debt, Department of the Treasury, Washington, D.C. 20239.

Treasury notes and bonds pay interest twice a year. Minimum denominations for notes: $5,000 for those maturing in less than four years, and $ 1,000 for those maturing in four years or longer. The minimum denomination for Treasury bonds is $1,000.

18

HIGH-GRADE CORPORATE BONDS

Once upon a time, high-grade corporate bonds were so safe, they were *dull*. These days, alas, even sound bonds from large, prosperous companies can be perilous. Let's look at the risks:

Interest-rate risk. If interest rates rise, the current value of your bonds will decline. The longer the term of your bonds, the more their current value will sink if interest rates climb. Of course, if interest rates *fall*, your bonds will be worth more. To realize any loss or gain, you would have to sell the bond before maturity. If you hold on, you should receive your original investment back. But if interest rates have risen, the interest you receive from your bonds while you're waiting for them to mature will be relatively low.

To reduce interest-rate risk: Diversify your maturities. Or keep your maturities short-term (one to seven years) and intermediate-term (seven to 15 years). Long-term bonds mature in 15 or more years. The truism among bond-fund managers: "Long . . . and wrong."

Credit risk. The company that issued your bond may get into a jam, and its credit rating—and the value of your bond—may plummet.

To reduce credit risk: Concentrate on bonds rated AAA, AA, or A by Standard and Poor's Corporation. Usually the higher the yield, the lower the rating. And diversify: Don't have more than 5% of your portfolio in any one issue.

Call risk. Most issuers of bonds specify that they can redeem them before maturity—usually five to ten years after the bonds have been issued. You'll be paid a premium, perhaps a year's worth of interest. But issuers typically call bonds when interest rates have fallen; so you'll wind up with your principal again, and with interest rates in the basement.

To reduce call risk: Check the provisions before you invest. Don't buy a high-paying existing bond if it might be called soon. Consider buying an existing bond selling at a discount; the issuer will have no reason to call it.

Event risk. This includes all sorts of untoward events, such as the company's being taken over in a leveraged buyout, the new owner floating a lot of new debt, and existing debt being downgraded. When giant RJR Nabisco was taken over in 1989, the value of its bonds sank by about 20%.

To reduce event risk: Diversify. Or stick with utility bonds and Treasuries.

You can probably make more money by investing in individual bonds than in a bond mutual fund. But mutual funds give you diversification, liquidity, and stability—and an expert who can scrutinize all the risks listed above.

Offsetting the risks is the chief reward of corporate bonds: a higher yield than tax-exempt bonds, Treasuries, and certificates of deposit (of similar maturities), though not as high as low-rated bonds. Of course, the interest from corporates isn't exempt from federal or state taxes. And unlike CDs, you'll pay commissions to buy and sell them individually.

The longer the maturity of a bond, usually the higher the interest it pays. One reason is to compensate the buyer for tying up money longer.

Long-term bonds have proved disappointing over the past 40 years; inflation has ravaged their returns. But in the past 10 years, as inflation subsided, they did quite well indeed. And it may be that, in the future, bond buyers will insist on interest rates high enough to protect them against the return of soaring inflation.

Even so, circumspect investors will confine themselves to short-term and intermediate-term bonds. Usually the extra interest offered by long-term bonds hasn't been worth the extra risk. Two ways to play the bond market: (1) stagger your maturities, so you own bonds coming due a year or two apart and you can reinvest your money at current rates; (2) use the modified "barbell" approach—weight your bond portfolio heavily toward short-term and late-intermediate term.

In buying individual bonds from a stockbroker, concentrate on issues offered by blue-chip companies, which are listed in the newspapers. That way, you'll know that the market for these bonds is fairly liquid (you can buy and sell them easily), and you can check the commission your broker is charging. Usually brokers expect you to buy $25,000 worth of bonds at a shot, and they charge about $25 to $50 per $1,000 unit.

Use "limit" orders when buying or selling bonds. Specify the lowest price at which you'll sell, the highest price at which you'll buy. Most bonds are thinly traded, and trading just five or ten corporate bonds may push their prices up or down a few points.

19

HIGH-YIELD CORPORATE BONDS

"Junk" is another word for them. But there's junk and there's truly *squalid* junk, and you shouldn't confuse them. Some junk bonds are fairly presentable: Dr Pepper/Seven-Up, Duracell, United Airlines, Calvin Klein Industries, Compaq Computers, American Standard. Mutual funds like Vanguard High Yield incline toward presentable junk. And if you have a large portfolio of low-rated bonds inside a mutual fund, you're not assuming the hair-raising risk of someone who owns a few truly speculative junk bonds.

Even so, no one knows how badly the entire junkbond market will be hurt in a really serious recession. So, go easy—despite the fetching yields that junk bonds pay. Balance your high-yield bonds with high-grade bonds. And be sure that any mutual fund you *think* is a high-grade bond fund isn't really a high-yield fund. (Many funds buy both types.)

Then again, you may want to avoid junk bonds altogether. They're very similar to stocks, because their fortunes depend so much upon the short-term fortunes of the companies that offer them. And some authorities think you would be better off buying stocks instead.

If you can't resist the high yield of junk bonds, go the mutual fund route—and look for a fund that emphasizes higher-level junk (like Fidelity and Vanguard) as opposed to lower-level junk.

20

TAX-EXEMPT BONDS

Investors make a lot of mistakes when they buy tax-free bonds:

- They're not aware of the risks. A municipal bond is not a Treasury obligation; defaults can and do occur. In 1987, 123 issues worth $1.1 billion defaulted. That was more than the total number of muni defaults between 1972 and 1983. Before buying any munis ask a broker about their credit ratings from Standard & Poor's. Stick with those rated A or higher or those that are insured. Or diversify—buy ten or more individual bonds from different issuers, or buy into a mutual fund of tax-exempts.
- They're not aware of the "call" provisions—whether the issuer can pay off the bond early in case interest rates nose-dive.
- They're not aware of transaction costs. Especially for munis that are rarely traded, you may pay an enormous spread—the difference between the bid price and the offer price. To make sure you get a break, you'll probably have to invest a minimum of $50,000 to $100,000. You would also be wise to shop for the best price among several brokers.

Unless you have $100,000 or more and a reliable broker, usually you'll be better off investing in a mutual fund, whether you buy high-grade or high-yield munis—for the diversification and for the services of an expert manager. As mentioned, if you're considering any fixed-income mutual funds at all, investigate those offered by the Vanguard Group in Valley Forge, PA, which offers pure no-load funds with low expenses.

Whether or not you'll benefit from munis depends on your tax brackets, both federal and state. Compare what munis and taxables of similar maturities and credit ratings are paying now. Then check your "marginal" tax rate—the tax on the last dollar of your income. If your marginal rate will be 28%, for example, a taxable bond would have to yield 11.11% to equal a muni yielding 8%. To figure out the after-tax return, multiply 1 minus your tax bracket times your taxable yield. You must get at least this return on a muni to make it worthwhile.

Taxable Vs. Tax-Exempt Bonds

To equal a muni yielding . . .	5%	6%	7%
a taxable bond must yield (28% marginal bracket)	6.94%	8.33%	9.72%
a taxable bond must yield (31% marginal bracket)	7.25%	8.70%	10.15%
a taxable bond must yield (33% marginal bracket)	7.46%	8.96%	10.45%
a taxable bond must yield (36% marginal bracket)	7.81%	9.38%	10.94%
a taxable bond must yield (39.6% marginal bracket)	8.28%	9.93%	11.59%
a taxable bond must yield (42% marginal bracket)	8.62%	10.34%	12.06%
a taxable bond must yield (46% marginal bracket)	9.26%	11.11%	12.96%

If you pay high taxes to your state, a bond or fund that invests exclusively in your state's bonds might be a good choice. Bonds issued by the territories—Puerto Rico, the U.S. Virgin Islands, and Guam—are exempt from taxes in most states. Three states currently tax all interest from muni bonds, within or outside the states: Illinois, Iowa, and Wisconsin. The District of Columbia and five states don't tax any muni bond income: Indiana, Nebraska, New Mexico, Utah, Vermont. States without income taxes: Alaska, Florida, Nevada, South Dakota, Texas, Washington, Wyoming. State legislatures change their minds readily, so double check before making any investment decision.

21

ZERO-COUPON BONDS

Zero-coupon bonds are like U.S. Series EE Bonds (see Key 16). You invest a relatively small amount of money, and after a certain number of years—1 to 30—you receive a relatively large amount of money. That is, you buy these bonds at a discount.

With individual bonds, you cannot reinvest interest; with unit investment trusts, if you *can* reinvest interest the price may be different. With zeros, though, you know exactly what sum you'll receive on a particular date.

The interest from zeros accumulates, and you get all of it in one fell swoop, at maturity. You can buy a $1,000 zero for as little as $100 or $200, depending on when it comes due and what the yield is. So, if you want to have a certain amount of money on a certain date—during the year or years you retire, say—zeros are a nice way to go.

There are three main types of zeros:

Corporate bonds. With these, you will pay Uncle Sam taxes on the interest you *don't* receive every year—the "phantom" interest. Stick with corporates rated highly by Standard & Poor's—AAA or AA. And be warned that corporates may be paid off before maturity.

Municipal bonds. Here, you need pay no taxes on the phantom interest. Stick with high-rated tax-exempts. Again, be aware that these can be called before maturity.

Treasury obligations. Here, you pay federal, not state taxes. You can buy STRIPS, as they're called, directly from the Treasury—and they're the only zeros that are unlikely to be called. Maturities are typically 30 years.

Of course, if you have corporate or Treasury zeros inside a tax-advantaged retirement plan such as an IRA, you will defer paying any taxes on the phantom interest.

Curiously, with a few corporate bonds you don't have to pay taxes on phantom interest. Examples: General Motors Acceptance Corp. bonds maturing in 2012 and 2015, and Exxon Shipping Co. bonds of 2012. These bonds were offered before Congress ruled that interest from corporate zeros is taxable every year.

The price of a long-term zero can fluctuate, depending on current interest rates. A 30-year zero Treasury, for instance, is 2.5 times more volatile than a 30-year Treasury bond. So, unless you're playing the interest-rate game, plan on holding a zero until maturity.

You can buy zeros through brokerage firms or through two mutual funds, Benham Capital (1-800-227-8380) and Scudder (1-800-225-2470). With mutual funds, you just specify the target date. Both Benham and Scudder are no-load funds with low expenses. Those expenses can mount up over the years. So, with a long-term zero, you may be better off paying a broker a commission for individual issues or buying STRIPS directly. Shop at different brokers, and inquire about the prices of zeros maturing at around the same time—1998, 1999, and 2000, for example. Two major discount brokers, Charles Schwab and Fidelity Investments, charge competitive rates.

For the best values, you might choose the zero with the highest yield to maturity, which may *not* be the zero with the longest maturity. As with all bonds, you may be wise to "ladder" your investments—buying zeros every few years, just in case interest rates rise.

Here's how to figure out what sum of money you will receive from a zero:

How to Get $1,000
Yields

Years from Retirement	6%	7%	8%	9%	10%
18	$345	$290	$244	$205	$173
13	464	409	361	318	281
8	623	577	534	494	458

Let's say that you're 50 and you want $50,000 when you're 63. The current yield on a zero is 10%. You would buy 50 times $281, or $14,050, worth of zeros.

22

FIXED INCOME MUTUAL FUNDS

Try to avoid stockbrokers when you buy fixed income mutual funds. The yields on these funds aren't especially high, so a broker's commission can really hurt you—especially a 5.5% or 8.5% commission. Buy such funds directly from mutual fund families like Vanguard, Fidelity, Scudder, Dreyfus, Neuberger & Berman, and T. Rowe Price. And avoid any fund that has high expenses, a chief component of which is a 12b-1 fee (a special charge that some funds assess to pay marketing costs). These fees range from 0.25% to 1% of assets every year. A fee of 0.25% isn't terrible; a fee of 1% a year *is*. And avoid any fund that charges you commissions when you reinvest your interest.

Know what you're buying. Is it a fund that invests in high-grade bonds or low-grade bonds? Find out whether the fund can switch from one strategy to another, so that one month the fund is concentrated in the bonds of IBM and other blue chip companies, and the next month the bonds of companies hardly anyone has heard of—or would want to—dominate the portfolio.

Don't buy *any* fixed-income fund if you don't understand the underlying investments. For example, government-backed mortgage securities pay better than Treasuries, even though they're almost as safe. But they have one big drawback: If interest rates go down, the mortgagors might pay off their loans early—and the yields on your mortgages could sink.

Also check the maturities of the fund's holdings before you buy. Don't be guided by what the spokespeople for a fund tell you: Different people, for example, define "short-term" differently. It may be one year, one to three years, or one to five years. Inquire about the numbers. The shorter the average maturity, of course, the less volatile the fund.

As mentioned in Key 12, focus on a fund's recent total return, not on the current yield.

A unit investment trust can be suitable for conservative people. You get diversification along with the assurance of receiving your original investment back, or close to it, at a certain time. The portfolio of securities is unmanaged, so there are low expenses. (If a bond is near default, though, the managers can replace it.) On the other hand, you'll pay 4%–4½% commission up front. Some of the bonds may be called (paid off early), so your yield might fall.

Also consider closed-end bond funds selling at discounts to their net asset value.

Finally, as previously mentioned, compare any fixed-income fund you're thinking of buying with a similar Vanguard fund. Vanguard funds are no-loads and have low expenses. For the names of good fixed-income funds, see the Appendix.

23

STOCKS

The stock market is dangerous. It is especially dangerous for older people, who may not have the time or the financial resources to wait out the usual market declines The stock market is *wildly* dangerous for older people who are unsophisticated about investing.

Making money in the stock market may seem easy: After all, the long-term direction of the market is way up. So all you have to do, supposedly, is buy good stocks and hang on.

But if you ask a random assortment of people whether they've made or lost money in stocks, chances are most will admit they've lost money—the honest ones, that is. Why? Because they may have bought good stocks at prices that were too high. And, instead of hanging on, they sold in a panic as soon as the prices dropped a bit. (The rule is that the first stock you buy always loses money.) If you've always invested in CDs or money market funds where you never lose money, losing money in stocks—even temporarily—may throw you for a loop.

No matter how smart or confident you are in your general abilities, be scared of the stock market. The older you are, the less you can afford to learn from expensive mistakes. And the stock market can be bewildering, rising when you expect it to fall, falling when you expect it to rise. The market seems to always do whatever makes the greatest number of people look foolish.

Yet a portion of your portfolio typically *should* be in stocks—simply because, despite their volatility, they can bless you with enormous profits.

To boost your chances, here are some rules to follow:

Hire an expert. No, *not* your local stockbroker, but a professional money manager with a good record—like

Michael Price at the Mutual Series, Robert Sanborn at Oakmark, Richard Strong at Strong Total.

Diversity. Don't hold just a handful of stocks; hold a basketful in different industries. It may be tempting to buy a few electric utilities, with their high dividends and stability. But you'll be safer buying into a stock mutual fund—even a fund that invests in a wide variety of electric utilities. If you want to play it especially safe, consider a mutual fund that invests in bonds as well as stocks, or a fund that concentrates on high-dividend stocks. Check how volatile a fund has been in comparison with one of the stock market indexes like the Standard & Poor's 500. (See Key 7.)

Choose wisely. Invest in a mutual fund with a good track record and with an investment strategy that you understand. If you have the confidence, bypass a stockbroker or financial planner and invest directly in a no-load or low-load mutual fund—one without high sales charges. (See Key 24.)

Dollar-cost average. Don't invest a huge chunk of your money in the stock market all at once. Put regular amounts into the market over a period of time—so that you'll likely wind up with an average price, rather than a high price. If you want to invest $10,000, for example, you might invest $2,500 every three months over the course of a year. By dollar-cost averaging, you'll also manage to buy the most shares of a stock when prices are low—just when you *should* buy them.

Develop a strategy . . . and stick to it, if you're going to invest in individual stocks. The two main strategies are (1) buying stocks cheap (when their price-earnings ratios are unusually low, or when the ratio of their price to their book value is low); and (2) buying the stocks of growing companies before other investors have discovered their appeal (one sign: few institutions, like pension plans and mutual funds, own the stock). If you don't know how to determine whether a stock's p/e ratio is low, or how to find out the ratio of a stock's price to book, or what a low ratio is, or how to learn the number of institutions that own shares—invest in stock mutual funds rather than individual stocks until you find out.

24

STOCK MUTUAL FUNDS

While stock (or "equity") funds provide you with diversification and with a professional manager, they can be bewildering. There are so many choices—of different funds, of different *kinds* of funds. Besides, surprisingly, it can be difficult to identify a fund with an indisputably excellent track record.

For the retirement-minded, though, the choice clearly should be conservative, stable funds that have established good records over three- and five-year periods. Ideally, they should also be no-load or low-load funds—those that don't charge high commissions.

The simplest way to invest in a stock fund is by means of an *index* fund—one that mirrors a model of the stock market as a whole. One well-known replica of the market is the Standard & Poor's 500—500 stocks in a variety of industries, typically big company stocks. Very few portfolio managers manage to beat the S&P 500 regularly. Many underperform the S&P 500 regularly.

A fund with low expenses and no sales charges that mirrors the S&P 500 is Vanguard Index Trust 500 Series. You can buy shares for a minimum of $3,000; call 1-800-662-7447. By buying its shares, you are assured of truly wide diversification—and that your investment will almost keep up with the market itself. (Expenses will keep the fund's returns a little below the S&P 500.)

Another conservative choice would be a *market-timing* fund, which shifts the percentages of its stocks, bonds, or other investments according to where the managers believe the various markets are heading. Vanguard Asset Allocation tilts toward stocks, but has enough invested in bonds to make the fund's price per share (net asset value) more stable than the S&P 500. Other mutual-fund families, like Fidelity, also offer market-timing funds—which they may call asset allocation funds.

A true *asset allocation* fund invests in more than just stocks, bonds, and cash equivalents. Typically, such a fund has part of its money invested in precious metals, real estate, and foreign stocks as well. These other investments may shine if domestic stocks sink or if inflation roars back. If asset allocation funds don't go overboard in switching their holdings, they can be a good conservative choice. USAA Cornerstone (1-800-531-8000) invests in gold stocks, foreign stocks, real estate stocks, government securities, and stocks that seem undervalued.

Still another conservative choice is a *balanced* fund, which buys both stocks and bonds. Example: Wellington (1-800-662-7447), which tilts heavily toward stocks.

An *equity-income* fund invests mainly in high dividend stocks, like blue chips and utilities. An example is Fidelity Equity-Income II (1-800-544-6666). A *growth-and-income* fund invests in both growing companies and high-dividend payers. Example: Mutual Beacon (1-800-448-3863).

A *total-return* fund can be another conservative choice. Such a fund is a balanced fund with a broad mandate: It can emphasize either stocks or bonds, depending on which market the managers believe has the better outlook. Example: Strong Total Return (1-800-368-1030).

Finally, any stock fund with a history of low volatility and high returns is a candidate for your portfolio. Lindner Dividend (314-727-5305) is an example.

Volatility can be measured by comparing a fund's price fluctuations with the S&P 500. The index is given a beta of 1. A fund with a beta of 0.80 is only 80% as volatile. Another way of measuring a fund's fluctuations is to track its ups and downs over time—its standard deviation. The S&P 500 has a standard deviation of 10%. A fund with a standard deviation of 4 is significantly more stable.

Now let's check the standard deviations of some of the funds we've mentioned:

Fund	Type	Standard Deviation
Fidelity Equity-Income II	stock income	7.5
Fidelity Puritan	balanced	6.75
Mutual Qualified	growth & income	6.9
Lindner Dividend	income	4.85
Oakmark	growth	10.0
PBHG Growth	growth	21.7
USAA Cornerstone	asset allocation	7.4
Vanguard Index 500	index	8.0
Vanguard/Wellington	balanced	6.5

Source: *Morningstar Mutual Fund Performance Report,* January 1995.

Besides these types of funds, you can also invest in funds called aggressive growth (small companies, turn-arounds, special situations), growth (small and growing companies), foreign stocks, foreign and domestic stocks, precious metals, ethical investments, option income, various sector (like health care or broadcasting), and so forth. Still don't feel you have enough choices? There's another world out there—closed-end funds. (See Key 14.)

Evaluating funds. Few funds do well year after year. What if a fund has performed gloriously for the past three years but only average for the past 10 years? Would you buy it over a fund that has a fine 10-year performance record but only a mediocre three-year record? (Most experts would emphasize the more recent, three-year record as long as the ten-year record was not poor.)

Another complication: A popular way of evaluating funds is to compare their performances against the records of their peers—an income fund against an income fund, for example. But another reasonable way of evaluating a fund is to compare its performance against its volatility—the more volatile it has been, the better it should have done. Sometimes a fund that has lagged behind its peers has done very well indeed if you consider only its stability. A wonderful example is Valley Forge, a fund that mainly invests in money market instruments but occasionally buys shares of underpriced blue-chip stocks. Its performance has been poor compared to other funds, but its performance has been terrific considering its price stability—its standard deviation is an astoundingly low 4.35—making it attractive to conservative investors.

To play it safe, you might choose funds that have both kept ahead of their peers *and* performed well for their volatility. Check the standards that any rating agency uses. *Morningstar Mutual Funds* uses volatility ("risk adjusted returns").

How many funds? You should own at least two stock funds with divergent investment strategies. The two most popular strategies are (a) buying undervalued stocks, typically those with low price-earnings ratios (the basic-value approach); and (b) buying stocks of companies whose earnings have been growing apace (the momentum approach). We've already mentioned several funds that look for undervalued stocks. Two funds that follow the second approach are 20th Century Growth (1-800-345-2021) and Janus (1-800-525-8983).

When the basic-value strategy is working, the momentum strategy may not be—and vice versa. Perhaps investors turn to the momentum strategy when they no longer can find many undervalued stocks.

25

REAL ESTATE

The high returns of stocks, without the apparent volatility—it sounds as if real estate is the perfect investment. But it isn't. Real estate typically isn't liquid. And if it is liquid, the price may be volatile. You also may have to invest a large chunk of money to get a stake—and pay high commissions to boot. That's why some financial experts suggest that the average investor skip real-estate investments, apart from buying a personal residence.

You can invest in real estate without buying property in at least two ways: by means of real estate investment trusts (REITs), which trade on stock exchanges, and through real estate limited partnerships, which are sold by stockbrokers and some financial planners.

The trouble with REITs is that there's evidence that they don't go up when the consumer price index goes up; in other words, they behave like stocks, not like real estate, which traditionally has fared exceptionally well in inflationary times.

Real estate limited partnerships typically carry very high sales commissions costs. They can be difficult to evaluate, and many of them are simply terrible. If you try to sell your units prematurely, you'll face enormous losses. People nearing retirement should be wary of investing in such partnerships—and skeptical of anyone who recommends them.

As for mutual funds that buy the stocks of real estate developers and REITs, most just haven't fared well. And in any case, owning a few REITs in different parts of the country, with different focuses (commercial, industrial, residential), would seem to give you all the diversification of a real estate mutual fund.

Besides, any diversified stock fund can buy real estate stocks—and should, when they seem undervalued. And many companies not associated with real estate happen to own a good deal of real estate. So it may be true that you have enough real estate in your portfolio, even if you aren't aware of it.

If you're determined to invest in real estate, consider Fidelity Real Estate Investment, a mutual fund with a good record (1-800-544-8888).

But, as mentioned, if you own your own residence, you may have all the exposure to the real estate market that you need.

If you're house-rich but cash-poor, you might consider a reverse annuity mortgage.

With a reverse mortgage, you, in effect, refinance your house—get a new mortgage on it. You get (typically) regularly monthly payments for as long as you live in your home. Instead of you paying the lender, the lender pays you. In most cases, you must repay the loan when you move out or sell the house—or your heirs must repay the loan if you die.

What if you live on and on and exhaust the value of your house? What if the neighborhood deteriorates, and the value of your house nose-dives? If your reverse mortgage is federally insured, not to worry: The lender will be reimbursed for any loss. In newer programs without Federal Housing Administration backing, the lender absorbs any losses.

Reverse mortgages seem to have arrived. A 1992 survey for the American Association of Retired Persons found that 84% of older homeowners want to remain in their houses and never move.

Most reverse-mortgage lenders require that the borrower be 62 or older; that the house be all or mostly paid for; and that the residence not be a cooperative, condominium, or duplex.

The older you are, the more valuable the house; the lower the interest rate, the more you'll receive from such a mortgage.

Some borrowers ask for cash up front, to pay medical bills, tax liens, or whatever, and then for monthly payments. Most also want the payments to continue for as long as they remain in the house, not just for a certain number of years.

A borrower should be determined to remain in the house, and not retire elsewhere after a few years. In that case, the loan becomes expensive. A loan should be for the rest of your life. That's why 62 may be too young for someone who seeks a reverse mortgage; a person that age may want to move elsewhere. Other homeowners may be better off trading down and investing the difference for income. Still a third option: The homeowners sell the house to their children in return for a lifetime annuity—and continue living there.

For a free copy of "Home-Made Money: A Consumer's Guide to Home Equity Conversion," write to the AARP, Home Equity Information Center, 601 E. Street, N.W., Washington, D.C. 20049.

You can obtain a copy of Ken Sholen's book, *Retirement Income on the House,* for $24.95 plus $4.50 shipping and handling from National Center for Home Equity Conversion, Suite 155, 7373 147th Street West, Apple Valley, MN 55124. Sholen runs the Center. For $1 plus a self-addressed, stamped envelope, you can get a list of recent mortgage originators.

26

PRECIOUS METALS

After the stock-market crash of October 19, 1987, a wealthy investor telephoned the Lexington Goldfund in Saddle Brook, NJ. In a panic, he was thinking of selling his entire huge portfolio of blue chip stocks and putting all of the proceeds into gold. The fund's manager, Strategic Investments, to his credit, talked the man out of it.

As it happened, gold didn't soar after the crash—even though, traditionally, gold gains value in times of economic uncertainty. As ever, gold proved unpredictable.

Should you put 5–10% of your portfolio in gold, as many investors recommend? Not unless you're wealthy and feel you must diversify across all manner of assets.

The price of gold is extremely volatile. One mutual fund that invests in gold stocks, Lexington, soared 269.78% in 1993. The same fund lost 68.33% in 1992. Its 10-year annualized return: –4.74%.

And what happens when you put together gold's ups and downs over the years? You're back almost where you started. All you have accomplished is to keep pace with inflation. And you could have done that with Treasury bills or other cash equivalents—*without* gold's volatility.

Roger G. Ibbotson and Gary P. Brinson, authors of *Investment Markets* (1987), studied gold's long-term record and concluded that "most gold investors have only broken even in real [inflation-adjusted] terms." Still, they recommend that individual investors keep a "small" portion of their wealth in gold "in case of war, hyperinflation, or radical changes in the economic system."

As for silver, it's even more volatile than gold. And as for tangibles like furniture, art, etc., buy them only if you enjoy owning them. According to Ibbotson and Brinson, "they are not smart investments."

27

ASSET ALLOCATION

Many otherwise intelligent people have no idea what percentages of their assets are in stocks, bonds, real estate, or whatever.

Yet the *particular* investments you make aren't nearly so important as the *general* investments you make. That is, over the long term, your profit or loss depends more on what percentage of your portfolio you invest in, say, stocks, than on the individual stocks you buy. Over 90% of your total return depends on how your portfolio is allocated—not on whether you buy IBM or Genentech stock.

How you divide up your portfolio is known as "asset allocation." For those nearing retirement, obviously, high safety and high yields are likely to be paramount. When you're young, you're generally more able to accept the ups and downs of the stock market, knowing that stocks very likely will provide you the best returns if you hang on. But now you may not have the time, or the resources, to wait out a hibernating bear market.

Not that you should withdraw from stocks entirely. Stocks can help your portfolio keep ahead of normal inflation. And if you choose stocks with high dividends, or stocks of blue-chip companies, or mutual funds with excellent records, you'll combine high returns with a good degree of safety.

But don't turn your current portfolio upside down in a twinkling. Go slowly. It's dangerous to make drastic changes—buying or selling a huge chunk of stocks or bonds all at once. You might decide to buy stocks just before a day like October 19, 1987, the day of the Big Crash. To modify your asset-allocation model, use "dollar-cost averaging." You might revise your portfolio every three months, over a two-year period, to reach your new asset-allocation goal.

Your own asset-allocation model will depend not only on your age. Your overall wealth is also important: The more prosperous you are, the more volatility/risk you can assume. Something else to consider is your "risk tolerance": If an investment began losing money, would you panic and sell? Actually, "risk tolerance" is probably just another way of describing investment sophistication.

Every investment adviser you consult would probably recommend a different asset-allocation model. But here's a simple one from John Markese, research director of the American Association of Individual Investors:

Risk Tolerance	Stocks	Bonds	Cash
Five years or more from retirement			
Conservative	40%	30%	30%
Aggressive	60%	30%	10%
Close to retirement			
Conservative	20%	50%	30%
Aggressive	40%	40%	20%
At retirement			
Conservative	0%	50%	50%
Aggressive	20%	55%	30%

What if you're more than five years from retirement age? "I think very young people should have almost all of their money in equities, with a small liquidity reserve," Markese says. He recommends the stocks of growing companies—not, for instance, utilities.

The chart suggests that conservative investors might have nothing in stocks at their retirement. Markese himself believes that everyone should have some ownership of stocks. As he points out, "It's hard to maintain less than 40% in stocks and still have real growth—because of inflation."

The cash is for emergency money, so that you won't be forced to sell your long-term investments. "The less predictable one's income is," Markese says, "the larger one's cash balance should be."

"Cash," of course, means money market funds, Treasury bills, and certificates of deposit with maturities no longer than a year.

Another simple asset-allocation model—not adapted for those near retirement—is suggested by Larry Biehl, an investment adviser with Bailard, Biehl & Kaiser in San Mateo, CA:

Domestic stocks	20%
Foreign stocks	20%
Treasury bonds	20%
Investment real estate	20%
Cash	20%

Finally, a more complex model from Roger C. Gibson, an investment adviser in Pittsburgh, PA:

Short-term bonds	37%
Domestic stocks	18%
International stocks	12%
Domestic long-term bonds	10.8%
Investment real estate	10%
International long-term bonds	7.2%
Inflation hedges	5%

The term "inflation hedges" means gold and other precious metals along with oil, gas, and other "hard" assets. Gibson happens to think, by the way, that the asset-allocation model of a preretiree should not differ much from anyone else's. Because of the likelihood of continued inflation, he believes, even people well along in years should have a moderate exposure to the stock market.

A whole flock of mutual funds call themselves asset-allocation funds, but many are just market-timing funds—they try to be in bonds when bond prices are climbing and yields falling, in stocks when the market has started to climb, and in cash when yields on Treasuries and similar cash equivalents are unusually high. Even Vanguard's Asset Allocation Fund is only a market-timing fund: It holds stocks, bonds, or cash. A true asset-allocation fund holds a wide variety of investments typically including real estate, precious metals, and other inflation hedges.

Among the no-load asset-allocation funds are:

USAA Cornerstone: 1-800-531-8000 or 512-498-8000. The fund invests 18% = 22% of its assets in five categories: gold stocks, foreign stocks, real estate stocks, U.S. Treasuries, and undervalued stocks. Minimum: $1,000. *Morningstar Mutual Funds* rating: average.

Fidelity Asset Manager: 1-800-544-8888. The fund invests in stocks (10%–60%); bonds (20%–60%); and short-term fixed-income investments (0%–70%). Minimum = $2,500. *Morningstar* rating: highest.

Vanguard Asset Allocation: 1-800-662-7447 or 215-669-1000. The fund invests in stocks, bonds; and money market instruments, with no limitations as to the percentages. Minimum: $3,000. *Morningstar* rating: above average.

Obviously, investing in such funds spares you the time and effort of monitoring how your own assets are allocated and changing the percentages as time goes by.

28

PORTFOLIOS

Before assembling, or revising, your personal and retirement portfolios, decide how you want to allocate your assets. (See Key 27.)

- In general, don't make quick, drastic changes. Ease into, or out of, any particular market—stocks, bonds, money market instruments. Otherwise, you may put a large percentage of your assets into the stock or bond markets just before a big drop—or take out a large amount just before a huge gain.
- Keep things simple. Don't have so many stocks, bonds, or mutual funds that you cannot keep track of them all, and you dread the prospect of filling out Form 1040 come April.
- Do not keep your investments so simple that you assume too much risk. Don't own just one stock mutual fund, for example, even if it has a splendid record. Even the best money managers have off years. You would be wise having shares of, say, Fidelity Puritan along with shares of a similar fund, such as Vanguard/Wellington.

There are probably a few hundred different portfolios that would make sense for someone approaching retirement. Decide how much income you want or need and how much volatility and risk you can tolerate.

Let's say that you want your $100,000 in assets allocated 50% into stocks, 10% into money market funds, and 40% in bonds. Here's a simple portfolio:

Asset	Amount	Yield	Standard Deviation
Vanguard Index 500	$50,000	2.6%	10.09
Vanguard Bond Market	40,000	7.13	4.17
Vanguard Money Market	10,000	4.52	0

Your yield from this portfolio (as of this writing) would be 4.6%. The volatility would be far less than that of the stock market.

Now let's say that you want your $100,000 invested 40% in stocks, 50% in bonds, and 10% in cash equivalents money market funds, like money market funds. Here's another simple portfolio:

Asset	Amount	Yield	Standard Deviation
Oakmark	$20,000	0.9%	11.03
Mutual Qualified	20,000	3.7	7.25
T. Rowe Price Spectrum Income	50,000	6.6	3.74
Vanguard Money Market Prime	10,000	4.52	0

This portfolio would yield around 4.7% and have an average weighted volatility of 5.53—a little over half of the S&P's 10.

Incidentally, many stock mutual funds don't invest all their assets in stocks. They keep some in fixed-income investments or cash. You might have to tinker with your portfolio to bring it into line with your asset allocation model.

29

TAX SHELTERS

A few tax shelters continued to exist after the Tax Reform Act of 1986—municipal bonds and low-income housing, among them. But the very best tax shelter that's still alive is a retirement plan—especially one where your contributions as well as your earnings escape taxes until withdrawn.

True, you may be in the same tax bracket when you retire, or even in a higher bracket. But you may be able to time your withdrawals to lower the tax bite or, with certain retirement plans, take advantage of special forward-averaging. Meanwhile, you'll have had more money working for you.

Besides, you can lower your adjusted gross income by means of contributions to retirement plans, boosting your chances of being able to surpass the floors for medical, miscellaneous, and casualty deductions.

Finally, if your money is locked away somewhere, guarded by a fire-breathing dragon (the penalties you might have to pay for early withdrawal), you may be more of a mind to leave your nest egg undisturbed. Many people who invest in municipals for their retirement quickly discover how easy it is to dream up excuses to swipe cash from such an ill-guarded cache.

To demonstrate the blessings of tax-free compounding, let's assume that you invest $2,000 a year in a deductible IRA. We'll also look at a nondeductible IRA and a taxable investment, and assume that you're in the 28% bracket, so (for comparison purposes) your contribution is only $1,440 ($2,000 minus the 28% tax, or $560). We'll also assume that your money earns 8% a year.

Yearly Deposit:	$1,440	$2,000	$1,440
Year withdrawn (after taxes)	Regular Savings account	Deductible IRA account	Nondeductible IRA account
5th	9,984	10,564	10,025
10th	21,289	23,970	21,693
15th	36,247	43,667	37,891
20th	56,038	72,609	60,746
30th	116,875	177,628	140,384

Source: Arthur Andersen & Company

If you're 50 now, and plan to withdraw your money at age 65, the difference between investing $2,000 in a deductible IRA every year and in a regular savings account would amount to $7,420. That's over 20%.

30

IRAs

Obviously, you shouldn't put money into an Individual Retirement Account if you might need it soon. You face a 10% penalty if you take out the money before you reach 59½, unless you're disabled or withdraw the money in accordance with your estimated lifespan (as an annuity). You would have to keep a deductible IRA for about 13 years to overcome that penalty—about 19 years for a nondeductible IRA.

But withdrawing the money as an annuity is something for early retirees to consider. If you're 55 and can expect to live another 20 years, you can receive around $1,000 a year from a $20,000 IRA without penalty.

Nondeductible IRAs. Should you *ever* open a nondeductible IRA? You might, but you should consider municipal bonds instead. You can withdraw your money from munis without penalty, even before reaching 59½. And the earnings from most munis are *never* taxed. On the other hand, with a deductible IRA, you can invest in high-grade corporate bonds or Treasuries, which usually pay more than munis and may be even safer.

You should also consider annuities—fixed or variable. (See Key 35.) While you'll pay a penalty for early withdrawal of annuity money—to Uncle Sam as well as possibly to the issuer of the annuity—you can salt far more away than a mere $2,000 a year. On the other hand, there may be all sorts of fees connected with buying annuities.

Of course, if you can open up a deductible Keogh or SEP with your self-employment income, or contribute to a 401(k) plan where you work, put a nondeductible IRA on the back burner.

If you do go ahead with a nondeductible IRA, put it into the name of the spouse with less money accumulated in *deductible* IRAs. The reason is that when you withdraw money from a nondeductible IRA, you must apportion the money you withdraw from both your deductible and nondeductible IRAs. That means you'll have to pay taxes on money you put into your original deductible IRAs. (You pay taxes only on what your nondeductible IRA has earned, not on the principal.)

Deductible IRAs. Of course, if you can deduct your IRA contribution, go for it, whatever your age. The most you can salt away during any one year is $2,000, or 100% of your earned income, whichever is less. (Earned income doesn't include dividends, interest, and capital gains, but it does include alimony you receive.) You can deduct your contribution from your taxable income. And your money will grow, tax deferred, until you withdraw it—which you *must* start doing the April 1 after you reach age 70½.

You can deduct an IRA contribution, so long as you were not an active member of a tax-deferred, employer-sponsored pension plan during the year.

If you or your spouse do participate in a company retirement plan, you can still deduct your IRA contribution if your adjusted gross income (the last line on page 1 of Form 1040) was $40,000 or less. If you're single, or the "head of a household" for tax purposes, the cutoff is $25,000.

But don't give up the ship if you exceed those limits. If you're married, and your adjusted gross income is below $50,000, you can deduct *part* of your IRA contribution. The same holds true if you're single and your adjusted gross income is below $35,000. (In calculating your adjusted gross income, don't subtract IRA contributions.)

For every $1 that your adjusted gross income exceeds $40,000/$25,000, you lose only 20 cents of your deduction. If your adjusted gross income is $44,000, and you're filing jointly, you're $4,000 above the limit. Multiply the $4,000 by 20 cents, to get $800. Subtract $800 from $2,000. The $1,200 is what you can deduct. (You can still put an extra $800 into a *non*deductible IRA, for a total of $2,000.)

What if you're married, filing jointly, and your adjusted gross income is over $49,000—say, $49,500? Supposedly you can contribute only $100 to a deductible IRA. But the IRS, bless it, lets you deduct $200. Remember this $200 exception if you're single or the head of a household, and your adjusted gross income is over $34,000.

Spousal IRAs. Note, too, that if you earn at least $2,250 a year and your spouse doesn't work, or earns less than $250 a year, you can fund a "spousal" IRA, contributing a total of $2,250 into IRAs. You can put $2,000 in your name, or into your spouse's name, or $1,175 into each of your names. But you cannot put more than $2,000 into one account for that year. If you think you'll need the IRA money soon, put the bulk of it into the account of the spouse nearer age 59½.

Borrowing for an IRA. If you don't have the money to fund a deductible IRA, consider borrowing it: All the interest you pay on a loan to invest in an IRA is deductible (if you itemize) because it's investment interest.

Moving around IRA money. You can shift around your IRA money in two ways: by *transfers* and *rollovers*. With a transfer, you have your current custodian move the money into the hands of another custodian. You can do this as often as you like. With a rollover, you yourself get the money, and if you put it into another IRA within 60 days, you will escape a withdrawal penalty. A rollover gives you 60 days to play with that money, but you're limited to one rollover a year per IRA account. You're better off using a transfer. Have your new custodian handle the transaction.

Don't confuse this type of rollover with a "rollover IRA." If you get a lump-sum distribution from another retirement plan—from a Keogh, or from your employer's or savings pension plan—you can defer paying taxes if you roll it over into an IRA within 60 days of the distribution, using a trustee-to-trustee transfer. This type of rollover IRA *isn't* limited to $2,000 a year. (See Key 37, Payouts.)

IRA withdrawals. Unless you begin withdrawing your IRA money by April 1 of the year after you reach 70½, you will have to pay a penalty of 50% of the difference between what you should have withdrawn and whatever you did withdraw. If you take out a little at a time, you must have withdrawn it all by the end of your estimated lifespan. (Your IRA's custodian can provide you with tables showing the amount you must withdraw every year.) But the percentage grows smaller as you grow older, so you won't outlive all your money. (The longer you live, the longer your estimated longevity.)

There's a way to lower your required withdrawal rate. Name a younger beneficiary. If your spouse is your beneficiary, your estimated lifespans will be longer. (Two people can not only live as cheaply as one, but longer, too.) You can also name a beneficiary younger than your spouse—but you must assume that the age of your beneficiary is no more than 10 years below yours. (You can always use the real age of your spouse, even if he or she is over ten years younger than you.) If you change beneficiaries, though, the age of the first beneficiary still determines the payout schedule.

Contributing past age 59½. You cannot contribute to an IRA past the year when you reach 70½. But if your spouse is under that age, and unemployed, you can continue contributing on his or her behalf. If you're working, you can contribute to an IRA past age 59½, even if you have begun withdrawing money—not a bad idea, because your savings will grow tax-deferred and you can get at it without penalty.

Investing in IRAs. Don't put tax-exempt investments like municipals into an IRA. Not only would you be wasting the tax-deferral benefits of the IRA, but you wind up having to pay taxes on those supposedly tax-exempt munis! (Whatever emerges from an IRA is taxable.)

Also avoid antiques, art, collectibles, precious metals, gems, coins, and similar assets. Uncle Sam forbids them in IRAs—but makes an exception for gold or silver coins minted by the government.

You can open an IRA with a bank, brokerage firm, insurance company, or mutual fund. If you're young and inexperienced, you might start out with a certificate of deposit, just to learn the ropes. But then start investing in stock mutual funds. Most funds will lower their normal minimums for retirement money, simply because funds want money that's likely to remain there for years. Don't invest in single stocks with your $2,000 a year: The commissions will be high, the risk great.

It's probably a good idea to invest in undervalued-stock mutual funds in a retirement plan, as opposed to growth-stock funds. Undervalued stocks tend to pay higher dividends—taxable outside a retirement plan. They are also less volatile. And, in the long run, they have done better than the growth stocks. You can learn whether a stock fund is value- or growth-oriented by consulting *Morningstar Mutual Funds* or the *Value Line Mutual Fund Survey* in a library.

31

SIMPLIFIED EMPLOYEE PENSIONS

SEPs are sort of the lazy man's (or woman's) Keogh. With a SEP, you don't enjoy special forward-averaging when you withdraw your money after age 59½. You can put away less than you could into a money-purchase defined-contribution Keogh, or a defined-benefit Keogh.

So . . . why a SEP? Because you don't have to set up a SEP the same year for which you make the contribution, as you must with a Keogh. And because you can avoid the laborious filing requirements you face with a Keogh.

SEPs are like IRAs for the self-employed. You can salt away whichever is less, $30,000 or 15% of your net self-employment income, minus your contribution (which works out to 13.043%). You cannot set up a defined-benefit plan, only a defined-contribution plan.

Employers can set up SEPs for their employees if they have 25 or fewer workers and at least half participate. These SEPs work just like 401(k) plans: Employees can contribute over $9,000 per year. (The exact figure will change every year.)

As with all retirement money, you should diversify your investments. The younger you are, the more you should veer toward stocks; the older, the more you should incline toward fixed-income investments. You can invest a SEP with a bank, brokerage house, insurance company, or mutual fund; a mutual fund may give you the widest choices. You cannot put SEP money into art, antiques, collectibles, coins, precious metals, gems, and such. But you can invest in U.S. gold or silver coins.

Unless you're disabled, you cannot withdraw SEP money before reaching 59½; otherwise, you're subject to a 10% penalty. You must begin withdrawing assets from a SEP by April 1 after the year you reach 70½.

For the sole proprietor, the advantages of a Keogh outweigh those of a SEP—unless the amount of money is small. If you made only $1,000, for example, the difference between what you can put into a money-purchase Keogh ($200) and a SEP ($130 or so) may not be worth the extra effort.

32

KEOGH PLANS

For the self-employed, Keogh (HR-10) plans are usually much superior to IRAs and even SEPs. You can shield more money from taxes. If you file for an automatic two-month extension for filing your tax form, you can defer funding your Keogh; if you file early, you can wait until April 15 to fund your Keogh. And you can take advantage of special forward-averaging when you withdraw your money once you're past age 59½.

Drawbacks: Compared with IRAs and SEPs, the tax paperwork for a Keogh is a real pain. And you must have set up your Keogh by the end of the calendar year before the April 15 that your tax return is due. Also, if you have full-time employees, you may have to fund Keoghs for them, too. Finally, if your self-employment income is small—less than $10,000—you're probably better off funding up a deductible IRA, if you qualify. For example, with $9,000 in self-employment income you can put a maximum of $2,000 into an IRA, but only a maximum of $1,800 into a typical Keogh.

Still, the benefits usually outweigh the drawbacks. As with all retirement plans, you should diversify your investments. The younger you are, the more you should salt away into the stock market; the older you are, the more you should salt away into less volatile vehicles. You *cannot* invest Keogh money in art, antiques, collectibles, precious metals, coins, gems, or stamps. (And, just in case you were considering the possibility, forget about investing in 19th-century Rothschild wines.) Exceptions: gold or silver coins issued by the U.S. Government. Naturally, you shouldn't invest in tax-free investments— like municipals—because that would waste your tax advantages. (But some people do it.)

You can set up a Keogh plan with a bank, mutual fund, brokerage firm, or insurance company. You usually have the most investment choices with a mutual fund.

Keoghs come in two main flavors: *defined contribution* and *defined benefit*. With the first, your guide for what you can put in is what you earn; with the second, your guide is what you want to eventually receive.

Defined-contribution plans are divided into:

1. *Profit-sharing plans.* You can salt away whichever is less: $30,000 each year, or up to 15% of your net earnings—minus your Keogh contribution. (Just multiply your net income by 13.043%.) With a profit-sharing plan, you can vary the amount you put into a Keogh every year. You aren't forced to put in 13.043% or any money at all.
2. *Money-purchase plans.* You can contribute whichever is less: $30,000 or 25% of your net earnings, minus your contribution—which amounts to 20%. But while you can contribute more than you could with a profit-sharing plan, you *must* contribute the same percentage every year—whether you can afford it or not.

The solution is to have both. Then, every year, you can contribute .0909% (to your money-purchase plan) and zero to .1091% (to your profit-sharing plan). The two percentages add up to 20%. That will give you some flexibility: the choice of contributing from .0909% to 20% every year.

A defined-benefit plan is a complicated kettle of fish. What you can funnel away each year depends on what you want to withdraw every year after you retire, and *that* amount will depend upon your age, income, and life expectancy. The largest amount you can receive from a defined-benefit plan is $118,800 a year. Withdrawals of over $150,000 from all qualified pension plans may result in penalties. If you retire earlier than your Social Security retirement age (65 to 67), you're entitled to less.

Like a money-purchase plan, a defined-benefit plan forces you to make a specific contribution every year, whether or not you can afford it. That's why such plans are best for people in their fifties who are prosperous and have predictable incomes, like physicians. While you can salt away far more into a defined-benefit plan than into a defined-contribution plan, you'll have to pay an actuary to figure out the complex math.

You must begin withdrawing your Keogh money by April 1 of the year following the one you reached age 70½, either in installments or all at once. If you take your money out in a lump sum, you may get the benefit of a special forward-averaging formula. You must (a) be 59½ or older when you receive the lump sum; or (b) have been 50 or older on January 1, 1986. You cannot withdraw Keogh money before age 59½ and escape a 10% tax penalty unless you're disabled or unless you roll the money over into an IRA.

Even if you are salaried, you can set up a Keogh with your self-employment income.

33

401(k) PLANS

Along with money market funds, one of the most delightful financial innovations of recent times is the salary-reduction retirement plan known as a 401(k). If your employer offers one, congratulations. If you don't take advantage of it, think again.

- You can stash more money away into a 401(k) than into an IRA. The limit for a 401(k) in 1994 was $9,240. (The $9,240 will rise as the consumer price index rises.)
- Your contributions and your earnings aren't taxed—the same as with deductible IRAs. The money withdrawn from your salary isn't reported to the government as taxable income on your W-2 form, though it is subject to Social Security taxes.
- Your contributions lower your adjusted gross income, thus helping you to qualify to itemize (list all your tax deductions) and to pass the thresholds for deducting medical expenses (7.5% of your adjusted gross income), miscellaneous expenses (2%), and casualty losses ($100 per occurrence plus 2% of your adjusted gross income).
- Your employer may match your contributions to a certain extent and to a certain limit—20%, 30%, 50%, or even 100%. If your employer does help out, a 401(k) is irresistible. Your employer's contributions don't affect the yearly limit, but they count toward the 25% limit. And your other employer-sponsored pension plans also count toward the $9,240 limit for 1994.
- Unlike an IRA, you may be able to borrow from your 401(k)—such as for buying your first main home.
- Unlike an IRA, if you withdraw your 401(k) money in one lump sum after you reach 59½ (or 55, if you retire), you can use a special forward-averaging technique to

lower your taxes. But you must have belonged to the plan for five years.

Try to invest 10% or 15% of your income into a 401(k) plan. If your employer permits a 20% contribution, and matches it, go for it.

Warning: If you are highly paid, the highest amount that can be considered for contributions and benefits is $150,000. As recently as 1993, the highest amount was $235,840.

Your employer's contributions to all your "defined contribution" pension plans, though, are limited to 25% of your salary after your 401(k) contribution or $30,000, whichever is less. You may find that if you contribute less yourself, your employer can contribute more! Check with your personnel director. (A defined contribution plan focuses on what you put in, not on what you want to receive—as in a "defined-benefit" plan.)

Typically you can invest your 401(k) money into a money market fund, a guaranteed investment contract (which is like a certificate of deposit), a Treasury or bond fund, or a stock fund. If you're unsure, stick with the guaranteed investment contract. But the older you are, the more you should veer toward fixed-income investments; the younger you are, the more you should veer toward stocks. In any case, diversify.

Most 401(k) plans let you switch your investments periodically.

You may be able to withdraw money permanently from your 401(k) for financial hardship. But you must pay a 10% penalty on whatever you withdraw, before 59½, along with regular income taxes. *Withdrawals you make to cover medical payments that would be tax-deductible and exceed 7.5% of your adjusted gross income, or for disability, are not subject to this penalty.* If you're taking out money for financial hardship, you can permanently withdraw only the money you contributed, not your employer's contributions and not your earnings.

"Financial hardship" covers the purchase of a main home; next term's post-high school tuition expenses for you, your spouse, and your children; medical expenses;

and payments to prevent your eviction or foreclosure on your main residence. But your employer has a lot of leeway. To prove financial hardship, you must show that you have "immediate and pressing" needs, and no other resources meet your needs.

There's no 10% penalty if you *borrow* from your 401(k). But your employer may not permit it. If you can borrow, you must repay the loan within five years, unless you're borrowing to buy a home for yourself, in which case you will have more time; it depends on your employer, but usually it's the length of your mortgage, which might be as long as 30 years. The amount you can borrow depends on what you've borrowed in the previous year. You might be able to borrow money at below-market interest rates. If you're lucky, the interest you'll pay will go into your own account; otherwise, other participants will share it. (The interest is *not* tax-deductible.) If your 401(k) is $10,000 or less, you can borrow it all; otherwise, you're usually restricted to half, but not more than $50,000. In general, borrowing from your 401(k) is a bad idea.

If you leave the company and roll over the money into an IRA within 60 days, again there's no penalty.

Make sure that the trustee of the IRA gets the check, not you, or your employer must withhold 20% for taxes.

34

OTHER RETIREMENT PLANS

There are a bewildering variety of employer-sponsored retirement plants, with all sorts of permutations and combinations. Two pieces of advice: (1) Get to know your personnel manager; and (2) if you have a choice among plans, lean toward any in which

- your contributions, if you can make any, are before taxes;
- your company also makes contributions;
- you can make the highest contributions;
- the plan is liberal in letting you borrow, or make withdrawals (though you may face a 10% tax penalty on your earnings or whatever the company contributed);
- the investment managers have a good track record.

If you have a choice of investments, diversify; the younger you are and the more prosperous you are, the more you should emphasize stocks; the older you are, and the less prosperous, the more you should incline toward fixed-income investments, like Treasury obligations, fixed annuities, and guaranteed investment contracts. (See Key 27, Asset Allocation.)

Employer-sponsored retirement plans come in two main flavors: *pension* plans, where you normally cannot withdraw money unless you leave the company or retire; and *profit-sharing* plans, where you might be able to withdraw money before you leave the company—say, if you suffered a financial hardship, such as having high medical bills.

Pension plans are further divided into *defined contribution* plans, where the focus is on how much you can contribute; and *defined-benefit* plans, where the focus is on how much you will eventually receive. Typically, employees themselves don't contribute to a defined-benefit plan. Defined contribution plans may fare better, over the years, depending on how your money is invested—and you may be able to choose your investments. Defined benefit plans are safer, because there is a fixed, predetermined return.

With a profit-sharing plan, your employer may make contributions whether or not it has any profits. And it can vary its contributions.

All profit-sharing plans are defined-contribution plans. Subvarieties or cousins may be called employee *thrift* and *savings* plans; *stock-bonus* plans, where employees have the right to receive company stock, usually at a tempting discount and without normal brokerage commissions; and *employee stock ownership* plans (ESOPs), where employees invest mainly in their employer's stock.

If you do have a chance to buy your company's stock, consider how large the price discount is, the prospects for the stock, the current prospects for the market as a whole, and whether the stock's current price is unusually high or unusually low. Check the stock's rating in *Standard & Poor's Stock Guide* and in the *Value Line Investment Survey,* which should rank the stock both for its safety and on how timely a purchase it is now. And don't put all or even the bulk of your retirement money into your company's stock—diversify.

"Vesting" means that you're forever entitled to all the money in your retirement plan. How many working years it takes before you're vested depends on the terms of the plan.

If you withdraw your money from a company savings plan before you reach 59½, you will face a 10% tax penalty unless

- you use the money to pay deductible medical expenses;
- you're 55 or over and take early retirement;
- you're disabled;
- you leave the company, take your savings-plan money as an annuity, and the company's retirement plan sets 55 as the normal age of retirement;

- you leave the company and roll over the money into an IRA or into another company's tax-deferred retirement plan.

   (Your employer must withhold 20% of the money unless you make a trustee-to-trustee transfer; you don't have possession of the money yourself.)

   For advice on withdrawals, see Key 37, Payouts.

Teachers and other employees of nonprofit organizations can save for their retirement with a 403(b) or 403(b)(7) plan. The first is for annuities; the second includes investments in closed-end and open-end mutual funds. Like a 401(k) plan, your contributions are tax-deductible and your earnings are tax-deferred.

Either your employer contributes to your 403(b) plan, or you do, through a payroll deduction. The limits on what you can stash away are complicated, but they are more generous than with a 401(k) plan or an IRA—which is why they are even more desirable.

35

ANNUITIES

Annuities are both a way to save for your retirement and a way to receive retirement money. If you're using an annuity to save, it's a *deferred* annuity. If you're buying an annuity to receive a yearly stipend for as long as you live, it's an *immediate* annuity.

These days, annuities have become especially popular, and with good reason. Now that IRAs may not be deductible, why not go with an annuity? Annuities also enjoy tax-deferred growth. You can sock far more away into a nondeductible annuity—a minimum of perhaps $1,000 and with virtually no maximum. And you will avoid the record-keeping bother of having both deductible and nondeductible IRAs.

Not that annuities are perfect. For example, the insurance company that issues the annuity may penalize you as much as 7% for early withdrawals—typically within the first five years after you buy the annuity. Even if an insurance company lets you withdraw part or all of your original contribution without penalty, there's a 10% IRS penalty if you withdraw money from an annuity before you reach age 59½. Also, some annuities have high fees—because of 4% sales commissions, administrative costs, and "mortality and risk-expense guarantees," which help cover the company in case a policyholder dies before the annuity begins paying out. The heirs are then entitled to the full original deposit, even if it has declined in value.

You can buy an annuity in one lump sum *(single premium)* or make payments over the years *(flexible payment)*. Thomas B. Gau, a CPA and CFP in Torrance, California, reports that the single-premium variety usually offers better terms.

Annuities can be invested in either a bond (*fixed*) or in a variety of mutual funds (*variable*). The mutual funds can be stock, bonds, money market funds, even real estate, and your principal may fluctuate (though not, of course, in the case of money market funds). The bonds in a variable annuity will be a variety and the fund managers may shift their investment grades and their maturities; the bonds in a fixed annuity will be pretty much unchanging.

The trouble with the older fixed annuities was that if interest rates rose, you were generally stuck with a low interest rate. These days, though, you can purchase a fixed annuity where the interest rate remains competitive because it may be readjusted every year or even every few months.

In choosing a fixed annuity, look for one with low expenses. Low-cost fixed annuities are offered by USAA Investment Management in San Antonio, TX (1-800-531-8000). Check any fixed annuity you're considering with one from USAA. Also look for a fixed annuity whose early-withdrawal fees vanish in five or six years, and that offers a high initial interest rate, but not just for a short time. Beyond that, make sure that the insurance company issuing the annuity gets an A+ rating from A. M. Best & Company. Check that your contract has a clause allowing you to cash out if the insurance company lowers your interest rate much below your original rate—for example, 1%. And be wary of an annuity with a large percentage of its investments in low-grade bonds.

For variable annuities, check into a family of funds with good track records—like Fidelity, Neuberger & Berman, Scudder, and Merrill Lynch. You cannot buy a fund open to the general public through a variable annuity. But you can buy clones of famous funds. Only the names are different. Two fund families that offer low-cost annuities with no early-withdrawal penalties are Vanguard (1-800-462-2391) and Scudder (1-800-242-4402).

Variable annuities have the potential to return far more than fixed annuities, but—especially in the case of stocks—they subject you to more risk. Also, your choice of investments may be relatively small, and your opportunity to make tax-free exchanges from fund to fund may be limited to various times of the year.

For older, more conservative people, fixed annuities may be the better choice. But if you have five to ten years before you'll need the money, consider a variable annuity invested in a stock mutual fund with a good record.

For a discussion of withdrawing money from annuities, see Key 37, Payouts.

36

LIFE INSURANCE

Life insurance is intended to protect your dependents in case you die and your regular income disappears.

The person who needs life insurance the most is young, with little in the way of an estate, and with a regular income that other people depend on—spouse, children, parents, siblings.

As your children grow, become educated, and leave home, and as your assets grow, you can cut back on your coverage. You don't have to drop your policies. Just ask your insurance company what the premium would be on less coverage—$50,000 and not $200,000, say—and decide how much coverage you really need to buy.

Once your estate is large enough to support your spouse or other dependents, you may not need life insurance at all. And the nest egg you need will be less than what *both* of you would need to retire on—50% to 75% of a two-person retirement nest egg.

Debra Morrison, a CFP in Fairfield, NJ, points out that you may want life insurance to lessen the bite that your heirs will pay in estate taxes.

The rule of thumb on how much life insurance you need is five or maybe seven times your yearly income. As a rule of thumb, it's not bad—for young people. But it doesn't apply to people who have already built up a sizable estate.

Estimating how much you should have is like figuring out the nest egg you'll need when you retire. A lot depends on your current net worth, your family and lifestyle, your personal dreams and desires.

If you died, is your spouse likely to remarry and thus have another income coming in? Does your spouse work, and could she or he work? (Many of the clients of

Graydon Calder, a financial planner in San Diego, don't want their spouses to feel forced to work or to be under pressure to remarry, so they opt for lots of life insurance.)

Do you want your children to work their way through public colleges, or to attend expensive private schools with the choice of not working?

In short, calculating the coverage you should have is dealing with smoke and mirrors. Ask two agents to figure out what you need, and one may say $200,000, another $500,000.

Still, you should make a ballpark estimate. A quick-and-dirty way: Total up all your assets available if you died—including possible Social Security payments for your spouse and children. Then calculate what they would need every year. Include an amount for a college fund. Finally, figure out what sum—before taxes—would provide a return (at a reasonable interest rate) that would close the gap, based on your spouse's life span plus ten years, and your children's age after graduating from college.

Besides how much life insurance you need, another tough question is, What kind? Your major choices are term, universal, variable life, and variable universal. Actually, all policies are either term or variations on term, which is simple insurance, like the insurance on your house. The others combine term with a savings account—a "cash value."

Graydon Calder, who is also a chartered life under-writer, says that when he started out as a financial planner in 1961, "I was a great advocate of buying term and investing the difference." (Term is much cheaper than whole life because you don't have a savings account and because the premiums are low when you are young and, generally, need more coverage). He recommended "declining" term—so coverage would go down as his clients' other investments appreciated. But he's changed his mind. He still believes in buying term and investing the difference—but now he recommends "level" and not decreasing term. That way, his clients have more flexibility in deciding how much insurance they need.

The trouble with buying term and investing the difference is that, as Thomas B. Gau notes, "Most people buy term and *spend* the difference." Or if they do invest the difference, they do so unwisely or unluckily, and their estate remains where it was. Joseph Mintz of Dallas agrees. "I'm no 'term-ite.' I do think whole-life is highly inefficient, but I've seen people who bought it wind up with big estates—$700,000 or $800,000—that they might not have had otherwise."

That's why it's important to have a yearly insurance checkup. If your assets aren't growing, consider switching from term insurance to whole life *before* the premium becomes excessively expensive. You'll be forced to save—and enjoy the tax-deferral of the earnings on your cash value as well.

Universal life is a big improvement over traditional whole life. The returns are "interest-sensitive"—closer to current rates. Salespeople's commissions are lower. You can adjust your premium payments, stressing either insurance or savings. (While some whole life policies are interest-rate sensitive, they are not nearly so flexible as universal life.)

As for variable life insurance policies, they can be fine investments. (If you're only saving for retirement, a variable annuity makes more sense because you don't have to pay for any life insurance). Still, if you could use more insurance, consider variable life. Your first step is to find a mutual fund family you admire, then see whether you can buy its funds through a variable policy. Fidelity and Neuberger & Berman offer such policies.

In buying insurance, stick to companies rated A+ by A. M. Best & Co. Says Gau, "A+ companies may charge no more than A companies, so why not go for A+?"

Policies: Costs and Benefits

Policy	Premiums	Death Benefit	Cost
Term	Increase as you grow older	Fixed	Lowest
Whole life	Fixed	Fixed	Highest
Universal Life	Flexible	Flexible	Moderate
Variable	Fixed	Varies, with a minimum	High
Variable Universal	Flexible	Varies, with a minimum	Moderate

37

PAYOUTS

You need expert guidance whenever you're eligible to receive an enormous pile of money—e.g., a distribution from a tax-deferred pension plan, Keogh, 401(k), or 403(b) plan. Don't go it alone. Mistakes can be costly.

You can take at least one of three steps: move the money into an IRA within 60 days, via a trustee-to-trustee transfer, so it continues to grow, tax-deferred; take the money as an annuity; or accept the money in a lump sum, where you receive the entire balance in one year. Lots of people love getting lump sums. It's so nice to receive a check for $100,000! And perilous. How much experience do you have investing $100,000?

Keep in mind that these three routes aren't mutually exclusive. You could combine them, transferring over part of your distribution into an IRA, taking another part as cash, and establishing an annuity with a third part.

If you follow the IRA route, or transfer the money into another qualified plan, your money will last the longest. It's usually the best step if you don't need the cash, since you face high taxes or a penalty unless you roll over the distribution. But bear in mind that money coming out of an IRA doesn't qualify for the special forward-averaging you can get from other retirement plans.

Warning: If you receive a distribution check payable to you, and you tend to invest it into an IRA, your employer must withhold 20% for taxes. Solution: Ask your employer to make the check payable to your new IRA.

If you put a distribution into a special "conduit" IRA, you can still move it into another company's qualified plan later on, and benefit from special tax treatment.

With an annuity, you'll have a choice. Do you want a "single life" annuity? Under this policy you will receive regular payments as long as you live, even if you live to be 869. A single-life policy pays the most. But if you die the payments will stop, regardless of whether or not you received all of your contributions back. (That's insurance: You win some, you lose some.) Also, if inflation ever roars back you may be in trouble—unless you have an annuity that adjusts the payout rate in line with current interest rates.

A "cash refund" annuity pays your survivor the balance of your total contributions if you die early.

You could also choose five- or ten-year "certain." This means that even if you die early, your survivors will be entitled to a full five or ten years of payouts. This is a compromise, so that your payouts will be less than from a single-life annuity.

Another choice is "joint and survivor," which covers both you and another person, typically your spouse. It pays less than a single-life annuity because two people have longer estimated life spans than one person. Once one spouse dies, the other receives 50% or 100% of the usual payout. If you choose 100%, naturally, your original payouts will be smaller.

While joint-and-survivor is a deservedly popular option, some people recommend going with a single-life policy and buying a life-insurance policy on yourself. If you predecease your spouse, your spouse will have the insurance money. You might also skip joint and survivor if your spouse already has enough money, or if you will need extra money during the early years of your retirement.

As for receiving your money in one lump sum, perhaps you must—because you have high current expenses. And perhaps you're sophisticated about investing and prefer managing your own money rather than just lazily receiving an annuity. In any case, you may be better off using forward-averaging on a lump-sum distribution, where the tax is not progressive: you pay five or ten times the tax (for a single person) on one-fifth or one-tenth the distribution. (The tax rate on one-fifth or one-tenth should be smaller.)

If you were at least 50 on January 1, 1986, you can use ten-year averaging or, if you prefer, five-year. With ten-year averaging, you'll use the 1986 tax rates, while the current lower rates prevail in five-year averaging. The ten-year averaging is usually better for amounts of $473,000 or less. Ask your tax adviser for guidance.

Immediately upon receiving a lump-sum distribution, you might put it all into a money-market fund or buy Treasury bills, then gradually move the money into your general-investment portfolio, using whatever asset-allocation model you have chosen. Or you can just follow the asset-allocation model you followed before.

Common Types of Annuities

Single life	Lifetime of annuitant only.
Joint and survivor 100%	Based on joint life expectancy, with survivor receiving 100% of former payouts.
Joint and survivor 50%	Based on joint life expectancy, with survivor receiving 50% of former payout.
10-Year Certain	Lifetime of policyholder, with a minimum of 10 years of payouts.
5-Year Certain	Lifetime of policyholder, with a minimum of 5 years of payouts.
Refund annuity	Lifetime of annuitant, with a refund to survivors if the payouts don't match policyholder's contributions.

Tax Treatment of Retirement Distributions

	Under 55	55 to 59½	59½ and older
IRA Rollover OK?	Yes	Yes	Yes

Spouse can also use this, with no penalty if over 59½.

10% Tax Penalty?	Yes	Yes	No

No penalty at any age if benefits are received as an annuity, or as the result of death or disability. No penalty between 55 and 59½ if distribution is from a tax-deferred pension plan as a result of your leaving your job.

10-Year Averaging?	If 50 before 1/1/86	If 50 before 1/1/86	If 50 before 1/1/86

You cannot use forward-averaging more than once.

5-Year Averaging?	No	No	Yes

You cannot use forward-averaging more than once.

38

SOCIAL SECURITY

Don't bank on Social Security to provide all the income you need in retirement. You should also count on your pension plans and your personal savings. But Social Security can typically provide 30% or more of what you need. The payments, by the way, are indexed to keep pace with significant increases in inflation (when the consumer price index increases 3% or more in one year).

In 1994, a 65-year-old single person who earned $60,600 or more a year could get a maximum benefit of only $13,764. A retired worker with a spouse who did not work might get a top of only $20,640. A married couple who both worked might get up to $27,528.

Social Security also provides hospital- and medical-expense coverage, via Medicare, once you reach 65; benefits for you and your dependents if you're unable to do any gainful work because of a physical or mental problem, or if your disability is expected to last (or has lasted) at least 12 months, or is expected to result in death; and benefits for your survivors if you die. Supplemental Security Income (SSI) is available for the blind, the disabled, and or to people 65 or older who are in financial need.

Born in	Age for Full Benefits
1938	65 Years, 2 Months
1939	65 Years, 4 Months
1940	65 Years, 6 Months
1941	65 Years, 8 Months
1942	65 Years, 10 Months
1943–54	66 Years
1955	66 Years, 2 Months
1956	66 Years, 4 Months
1957	66 Years, 6 Months
1958	66 Years, 8 Months
1969	66 Years, 10 Months
1960–	67 Years

When you can retire. For full benefits, if you were born in 1938 or later, you may have to wait until you're past 65.

Checking the record. These days, if you're close to retirement, you can obtain a good estimate of what payments you'll be receiving from the Social Security Administration. To receive a copy of the form to fill out, "Request for Earnings and Benefit Estimate Statement," phone either 1-800-937-2000 or 1-800-234-5572. You will also receive a list of earnings credited to your account. Make sure that the amount of your income that the SSA *could* tax matches the amounts you earned.

Do this every few years. You have three years, three months, and 15 days after the year in which you received your earned income to make corrections. (Mistakes *can* be corrected later, but not so easily.)

Do you qualify? To receive monthly retirement benefits, you must have reached retirement age—at least age 62. You must also file an application at your local SSA office. Do so three months before you retire, so you receive your first monthly payment promptly. Benefits are retroactive only for the 12 months before the date you filed, so don't delay for over a year. You'll need these records: a Social Security card, or at least your number; proof of age—a birth or baptismal certificate; Form W-2 for the previous year—or, if you're self-employed, your most recent federal tax return; and a marriage certificate, if you're applying for benefits as a spouse (a divorcee needs proof of divorce). For a child to receive benefits, he or she needs an SSA number and proof of age.

You must also be fully "insured." You must have contributed to SSA for enough quarters—three-month periods—to qualify. And you must have earned a minimum amount in these quarters. *If you have 10 years of work credit, or 40 quarters, you are fully insured.* Otherwise, the number of quarters you need depends on when you were born. That doesn't mean you'll get the *highest* benefits—only that you and your survivors are eligible for some benefits when you retire. For the *minimum* benefit, you must have six quarters.

The number of quarters you need for coverage depends on your age.

If you reach 62 in	You need work credits for this period
1989–1990	9 years, 36 quarters
1991 and on	10 years, 40 quarters

The amount you will receive depends on your average earnings over the years, and how long you contributed to Social Security.

Year of Retirement	Social Security at 65 Based on Maximum Earnings
1989	$10,800
1990	11,652
1991	12,240
1992	12,780
1993	13,416
1994	14,076
1995	14,952
1996	15,924
1997	16,944
1998	17,964
1999	19,092
2000	20,256

Should you retire at 62? If you do, you'll receive only 80% of your scheduled benefits at (currently) 65—your *primary insurance amount.* If you retire at 63, you'll get only 85%. At 64, 93%. These lower percentages will not change over the life of your benefits; you can't "unre-tire." (In 2000, those who retire at 62 will see their bene-fits reduced by 30%.) Besides, if you work until 65, you will probably have more higher earning years to your credit, which would boost your benefits.

The argument has been made that, if you choose to receive benefits at 65, you'll have to live to 77 to break even. But the life expectancy of someone 65 is 77, so it works out. (The people at the SSA aren't dumb.) But you might opt for 62 if you aren't in love with your job and have other, more pleasant things to do, can survive on reduced SSA payments, and are male—simply because men don't live as long as women.

If you work past 65. If you continue working past (currently) 65 and contributing to SSA, you'll receive an extra retirement credit of .25% a month, or 3% a year, when you do retire. In 1990, and every year after that, the 3% will increase by .25% each year until it reaches 8% in 2009.

But you may lose current benefits if you continue working. People receiving benefits lose $1 for every $2 they earn in excess of a varying base amount—$8,400 in 1988. Starting from 1990, the penalty is only $1 for every $3 above the base amount. When you reach 70, the reduction in benefits stops even if you continue working. (Beginning in 2000, that age will increase.)

Taxation of Benefits. Part of your SSA retirement benefits will be taxed if your gross income, half your SSA benefits, and any tax-free income exceed $25,000 if you're single, $32,000 for married couples. Your gross income in this case includes interest from tax-exempt municipal bonds. This is an argument for two older people who are receiving SSA benefits *not* to get married. Together, they could earn $50,000 and escape taxes on their SSA income.

Beginning in 1994, a new 85% inclusion rate may boost the amount of your Social Security benefits considered to be taxable income. The rate will apply to income over $44,000 for marrieds filing jointly or $34,000 for singles.

Benefits for others. If your spouse hasn't worked and isn't entitled to benefits on his or her own, he or she is entitled to benefits based on your coverage. At 65, the spouse would receive half of your primary insurance amount; at 62, 37.5%. If the spouse *has* worked but is entitled to less than half your primary insurance amount, he or she would nonetheless get 50% of your benefits. Otherwise, spouses are entitled to their own benefits.

If you retire and still have children or grandchildren who depend on you for support, they're entitled to half your primary insurance amount. A dependent child is one under 18, or a full-time student between 18 and 22, or a disabled child of any age if the disability began before age 22. A dependent parent who is at least 62 is also entitled to half your primary insurance amount.

If you die, whatever your age, your survivors who will qualify for benefits include your spouse at age 65 (or as early as 60, with reduced benefits—71% of your primary insurance amount); your unmarried children under 18, or up to 22 if full-time students; and your dependent parents who are 62 or older. A divorced, dependent spouse must have been married to the worker for at least ten years and must not have remarried (unless he or she was over 60 at remarriage).

Your unmarried children or grandchildren would receive 75% of your primary insurance amount if they would have qualified for 50% had you lived. Your dependent parents, if over 62, can also collect 75% of your primary insurance amount; if only one is alive, he or she can receive 82.5%.

Your widow or widower is entitled to a one-time $255 death benefit.

Your survivors, by the way, are entitled to benefits even if you weren't fully insured. But you have to be *currently insured*—which means that you earned at least six quarters of SSA credit in the three years before your death.

To request a statement of earnings, Form SSA-7004, from the Social Security Administration, phone 1-800-772-1213. You should check the figures every three years.

39

ESTATE PLANNING

Your "estate" consists of assets you leave when you die. "Estate planning" means, among other things, trying to dispose of those assets more in line with what you want, rather than what the law ordains, and saving on taxes along the way.

It isn't just the very wealthy who should plan the disposition of their estates, reports Paul R. Kenworthy, a certified financial planner in Minneapolis, MN. People of moderate means may need to do even more to minimize the tax bite and the usual legal delays.

A will is the cornerstone of your estate planning, but it does not cover everything. Generally excluded from wills are assets owned jointly, life insurance proceeds, and benefits from employment-related retirement plans.

Your assets may be subject to (1) federal estate taxes; and (2) state inheritance and estate taxes.

The federal government levies an estate tax on "taxable transfers"—money or property you have passed to someone else, either in the form of trusts or gifts while you are alive, or through distributions after death.

Only large estates are subject to the federal estate tax, but the tax bite can be enormous: rates can range from 37% to 55%. If your estate is over $600,000, you definitely should consider using trusts and balancing the ownership of your assets with your spouse. If you have lots of life insurance, you may easily surpass that $600,000, even without your knowing it.

Most states tax either your estate as a whole or the assets you leave your heirs individually.

There are two ways you can escape federal taxes:

1. The "free marital transfer." *Anything you leave your spouse is untaxed.*

2. Gifts. *You can give any person up to $10,000 a year.*
Thus, each parent could give two children each $10,000
a year, for a total of $40,000. At death, gifts made dur-
ing your lifetime that exceeded the yearly limit are
pulled back into your estate. Incidentally, for gift-tax
purposes, you need not count money spent for someone else's school tuition or medical care. Warning: Any
gifts you make within three years of your death may be
added back to your estate.

Even if you incur a gift-tax liability, you have a "unified credit"—currently $192,800—which can offset any
gift taxes you might owe.

The major tools in estate-planning include the following:

Your will. Your spouse also needs a will, even if he or
she has no assets. You may die before your spouse—and
your spouse may die shortly thereafter. If your spouse
dies intestate—without a will—his or her assets might be
disposed of according to the provisions of your state's
law, which might not be to your liking.

You should have your wills updated at any major
change in your life, whether it be a divorce, moving to
another state, a new child, a sudden increase in your
wealth. You can amend an existing will with a codicil.

While making your will, choose an executor and
guardians. An executor manages the estate until its assets
are distributed. You might name a relative as co-executor
with a bank or trust company. Also name people to serve
as guardians of your minor children, getting their permission first and checking the choices with your children,
if they're old enough to understand.

Martin M. Shenkman, a tax lawyer in Teaneck, NJ,
and New York, suggests that if you're giving away personal property—jewelry, a piano, and such—you *not*
include such bequests in a will. Have the will empower
the executor to follow your instructions in a separate letter. With a letter, "it's easier to change such bequests,"
says Shenkman.

Joint ownership. You and your spouse can own a
home, bank accounts, cars, and securities jointly. When
one owner dies, the property automatically passes to the

other. But there can be complications in the case of a divorce: Whereas wills can be changed easily, joint ownership cannot—unless both parties agree. And state and local estate taxes may be *higher* on jointly owned property. Also, joint ownership may be inadvisable in community-property states.

Gifts. An excellent way to protect your assets (below $600,000) from estate taxes. Some people consider $10,000 a year only a small amount of money. But if you and your spouse combine to present $10,000 a year to two children, that's $40,000 a year, $200,000 after five years.

Life Insurance. Usually the proceeds aren't subject to probate (where a court carries out your will), and they're also free from federal income taxes. If you assign ownership of the insurance to the beneficiary at least three years before your death, the proceeds can be removed from your estate. Debra Morrison recommends that large amounts of life insurance be owned by an irrevocable insurance trust to keep it out of your estate.

Trusts. These devices can help reduce your taxes and head off common financial problems. You can set up a trust through a will or through a separate document. With a trust, you transfer your assets to a trustee to manage for the trust's beneficiaries—who may be too young, too ill, or too inexperienced to manage them.

There are a bewildering variety of trusts. But the chief one is a *bypass* or *credit-shelter* trust, which allows you and your spouse to transfer up to $1.2 million to your beneficiaries, free of federal estate taxes, not just $600,000.

Example: A man has a net worth of $1.2 million. His will leaves the first $600,000 in trust for his wife during his lifetime, with the children inheriting the assets after she dies. The remaining $600,000 is left directly to his wife—free of federal estate tax because of the unlimited marital deduction. When she dies, the assets in the trust are distributed to the children, free of estate taxes, because the trust isn't considered part of the wife's estate. And if the assets in her own name are under $600,000, that passes tax-free to the children, too.

Another popular trust is the "charitable remainder unit trust", which enables you to give assets to a charity but keep the income from the assets for a period of time (such as your lifetime).

Beyond a will and trusts, consider a durable power of attorney. It gives your spouse, or someone else, the right to manage your affairs in the event you become incapacitated.

40

ADVISERS

Whichever *type* of adviser you choose, look for one experienced in dealing with the needs of people nearing retirement or already retired.

Several years ago I asked 20 advisers to physicians to rank the various advisers as to (1) their importance; (2) the difficulty in finding a first rate professional in the field; and (3) their ethics. Here's how they fared:

Most Important
Accountants
Lawyers
Financial planners/Money managers
Bankers
Average Importance
Insurance agents
Stockbrokers

Ranked below average were real estate agents, architects, and travel agents.

Clearly, the importance of advisers depends on their giving you continual guidance, not just sporadic advice that can make you, or lose you, a lot of money. The high ranking given to bankers, by the way, might surprise many people.

The next question was: In which areas is it especially difficult to find a top-flight adviser? In other words, where might Adviser A be far superior to Adviser B— and thus require that you do the most diligent search to find someone capable?

Hardest to Find
First-rate money manager
First-rate insurance agent

Finally, the question of ethics: In a conflict, which advisers put their best interests above your own? Which advisers would be most likely to recommend that you buy something inappropriate, just so they can collect a fee or a commission?

ETHICS RATINGS
Very High:
Accountants
High:
Lawyers
Financial planners
Bankers
Average to High:
Money managers
Average:
Travel agents
Insurance agents (property/casualty)
Average to Low:
Stockbrokers
Real estate agents
Low:
Funeral directors
Insurance agents (life)

By and large, it seems that an adviser's ethics depend upon:

- How prosperous the profession is—which in turn may depend upon how crowded the field is. (Funeral directors and real estate agents are in very competitive fields, and few earn sizable incomes.)
- How the advisers are paid. Those who receive commissions seemed to wind up way down on the totem pole.
- Traditional ethical standards. Life insurance agents and real estate agents seem to have inherited threadbare ethical standards; if you're skeptical, read the Machiavellian sales books written by these people for others in the field. (Personally, I would put lawyers in this category, too, despite their high ranking.)

41

CHOOSING
THE BEST

"There are not competent people enough in the world to go round," noted Bernard Shaw. "Somebody must get the incompetent lawyers and doctors." And, one might add, the incompetent accountants, stockbrokers, financial planners, and insurance agents.

Here are eight steps to take to avoid hiring a loser:

1. Decide what you need—and look for someone knowledgeable and experienced in that area. If you want investment advice, be dubious of hiring an insurance agent turned financial planner; if you want to know how to handle a lump-sum distribution, ask a financial planner or an accountant, not a stockbroker.

2. Become knowledgeable on your own. If you know something about taxes, or pension-plan distributions, you can more readily evaluate advisers' suggestions—and the advisers themselves.

3. Get recommendations. Distinguish between a "recommendation" (your source has used the adviser) and a "referral" (your source has a little list or has heard of an adviser named so-and-so). You can obtain recommendations from acquaintances or from business sources. And use your imagination. For the names of good lawyers, call a nearby law school. Ask lawyers for names of good financial planners or accountants.

Among the questions to ask: What are the adviser's strong points and weak points? Is he or she ever late with work? Are the fees the adviser quotes close to the final bills? Will the adviser refer you to someone else if a task is beyond his or her competence? Does the adviser do all the important work, and not slough anything off on an apprentice? Does the adviser keep you well informed? Or, to quote Roger A. Golde, author of *Can You Be Sure of Your Experts,* does the adviser "play the One Who Moves In Mysterious Ways, shrouding his views in professional jargon"? Above all, would you unhesitatingly hire that adviser again?

4. Do some research. Check with professional organizations—like the American Association of CPAs—to see whether any candidate you have is a member in good standing.

5. Look for credentials. Professional degrees and certifications show not only that an adviser is smart, but also that the adviser takes pride in the work he or she does. Membership in a professional organization is another good sign. Most associations have a standard of ethics and a continuing-education program. Besides, if an adviser does less than a proper job, you will have a place to lodge a complaint.

6. Look for experience. Hire the handicapped, if you will, not the inexperienced. Be wary of an investment adviser who hasn't witnessed a bear market, or a lawyer who hasn't drawn up many wills, or an insurance agent who hasn't learned a smattering about taxes. Of course, age shouldn't be your sole guide. A lawyer of 30 may have seven years of drawing up wills; an insurance agent of 60 may know nothing about variable annuities, just life insurance.

7. Set up a half-hour interview with at least three candidates. Check that they won't charge you for such a meeting—unless they give you concrete advice rather than merely answer general questions. Mention the names of people who recommended the adviser, so he or she knows you have people to complain to.

At the meeting, ask such questions as: What areas are you strongest in and weakest in? What experience do you have in the work I need done? Do you have a CFP or other professional certification? Who covers for you when you're ill or on vacation, and what are *that* person's credentials? Do you deal with the products of more than one company? Can you show me samples of your work (legal documents, financial plans) with the names of clients stricken out?

After the interview, ask yourself: Were the adviser's answers informed and logical? When he or she didn't know an answer, did the adviser avoid guessing?

8. Once you have decided on an adviser, ask for an engagement letter, which should specify the services to be performed, the estimated cost, the timetable, and what recourse you have if you are dissatisfied and wish to discharge the adviser.

Finally, give the adviser a trial. Let a money manager handle a portion of your money, or let an insurance agent evaluate your current coverage. And send courteous notes to other candidates you passed over. You may be seeing them again—soon.

42

REPLACING YOUR ADVISERS

If your stock portfolio began lagging way behind the Standard & Poor's 500, would you have enough confidence in your money manager to hang on? If the IRS called you in for an audit, would you have any qualms about your regular tax adviser's representing you? If your insurance agent recommended switching to another life insurance policy, would you be sure he or she wasn't just trying to wangle another commission?

The right time to evaluate your current advisers is: as often as possible. And as you approach retirement, you should not tolerate advisers whose competence worries you. Ask yourself:

- Do they still come up with fresh, useful ideas?
- Do they think well of one another—or do they habitually make snippy, disparaging comments about one of their number?
- Are all of them courageous enough to give you advice you don't want to hear—such as that trying to take a particular tax deduction is hazardous, or that a particular investment is too risky?
- Do they keep you up to date?
- If you paid more, do you believe you could obtain better advice?
- If an adviser weren't a personal friend, would you think more readily of replacing him or her?
- Do all your advisers successfully persuade you to take their advice? (If they're not forceful enough to persuade you, maybe you should hire people who can.)
- If someone asked you to name the best advisers in your area, would you unhesitatingly name your own?

If you're uneasy about any of your advisers, talk with that person—and check your grievances with your other advisers. Air your complaints: "My stocks aren't keeping up with the Dow." "You didn't return my phone call for three days." "You didn't tell me about the commission I'd pay on that mutual fund you recommended."

If the adviser doesn't resolve your doubts, your next step is to look for someone new. And once you find someone you have more confidence in, send your current adviser a note like this, which was devised by Boston lawyer Charles E. Westcott:

"The purpose of this letter is to advise you that I have decided to retain a new [type of adviser]. Effective the first of the month, [new adviser] will represent me. I would appreciate it if you will cooperate with [new adviser] toward an orderly transfer of your files and records.

"I appreciate your efforts on my behalf, and will promptly pay your statement for services that have been rendered to date. If you are agreeable, I may call upon you for special needs in the future. But I feel that my new firm may be more capable of serving my current needs.

"If you wish to discuss any aspect of the basis for this decision, I would be pleased to talk with you personally."

43

STOCKBROKERS

It's been said of stockbrokers that they can make you a small fortune—provided that you start out with a large fortune. Many an investor has also said that all their brokers ever did for them was make them broker.

Brokers are indispensable for anyone who buys individual stocks and bonds. A full-service brokerage firm can also provide you with useful literature and get you favorable executions (buying and selling at good prices). But brokers who are gifted money managers are likely to *become* money managers. The ones who don't become money managers on their own tend to be successful in proportion to their sales skills, not in proportion to their investment skills.

It boils down to the question: Whom do you want giving you investment advice—the manager of a top-performing mutual fund (Michael Price at Mutual Series, Robert Sanborn at Oakmark) or a friendly, chatty stockbroker? If you can pay enough, you could even hire a private money manager. (See Key 44, Money Managers.)

Yes, you'll pay extra to have an investment professional manage your money. But you're far more likely to wind up with a sound, diversified portfolio rather than a hodgepodge of stocks you bought on tips. And professionals have another advantage over stockbrokers: *They* aren't tempted to have you continually buying and selling, just to reap commissions.

As for stockbrokers who sell mutual funds, a beginner may benefit from their guidance. But check out the track records of any funds they recommend. Some brokers tout funds with inglorious histories, just for the sales commissions, the continuing fees they receive from the funds'

12b-1 ("distribution") plans, or the cut they receive whenever you reinvest any fund distributions.

If you can find a stockbroker who gives you good investment advice 60% of the time, you'll be very fortunate. Usually you will be better off sticking to mutual funds and professional money managers—especially at a time in your life when you can ill afford to make serious investment mistakes.

44

MONEY MANAGERS

If you have a lot of money to invest—$50,000 or more—consider a professional money manager. Why not just buy mutual funds instead? With a professional money manager, the argument goes, you may get more personal attention.

Usually money managers (also called investment advisers) charge 1% to 2% of the value of your total portfolio every year, not including the costs of buying and selling. Stockbrokers give "free" advice, of course. But money managers don't have the inherent conflict of interest of stockbrokers, who make money only when you buy or sell, and their track records are a heck of a lot better.

How can you tell whether a money manager's track record *is* really as good as he or she claims? The records they show you may be only for a few lucky accounts, or the records may exclude a bad year. And how can you tell whether any manager you choose will stay on course?

Hire a talent scout—someone who will find you a manager with an indisputably superior record, and make sure that his or her winning streak continues.

Several brokerage houses—Merrill Lynch and Paine Webber among them—will recommend advisers, who in turn may use the firms when they buy and sell securities.

But you may be better off hiring a completely independent talent scout. For names, write to Investment Management Consultants Association, 10200 E. Girard Ave., Suite 340C, Denver, CO 80231.

You usually must give a money manager the right to buy and sell securities for you without your approval—a "discretionary" account. You will still have to decide what investment strategy you want from a money manager, and how your assets should be allocated between stocks, bonds, and other investments.

45

ACCOUNTANTS

The trouble with many accountants is that they're accustomed to acting as referees, not coaches; they suffer from "analysis paralysis." You may look long and hard before finding one who will not only describe your situation, but will also tell you *what to do*—such as whether buying tax-free municipals is suitable for someone in your tax bracket, or whether you would be better off cashing in a particular certificate of deposit early, paying the penalty, and investing in a higher-paying CD.

Other accountants to avoid are the Milquetoasts—the kind who boast that they've never had a tax deduction disallowed and who are averse to any fresh ideas. "Accountants in general tend to reject change and innovation," claims Boston lawyer Charles E. Westcott. "Most of them have enough clients, and their business is comfortable and steady. So they feel that changes aren't necessarily in their own best interests."

On the other hand, you don't want a daredevil, either, the type who, to quote writer Howard R. Lewis, "waves red flags in front of the bulls of the IRS." In general, choose an accountant whose risk tolerance matches yours. As the saying goes, "Tax lions and tax mice don't mix."

Despite these warnings, accountants are among the smartest and most ethical of advisers, and their guidance can help you and your family enormously in keeping what you've earned, paying Uncle Sam only his fair share. More and more accountants are also functioning as financial planners, and for expert advice about everything from insurance to investments, such CPAs would be hard to beat.

CPAs have completed an accounting course of study in college, passed a 2½-day examination, and met their state's education and experience requirements. Accountants who aren't industry employees, but can work for individuals, are "public." A step below CPAs are public accountants—not certified. States vary in their requirements for public accountants.

In looking for an accountant, find out

- exactly what services he or she will provide—you want someone who will give you year-round tax saving advice and investment guidance, not just someone who will fill out your tax forms;
- where he or she obtained experience (a small or medium-sized firm is better than a giant firm);
- how many years of experience he or she has (seven or more is desirable);
- how many older clients the accountant has; and
- whether the accountant has the time to take on a new client. (If he or she is overtaxed, you may be, too.)

In dealing with an accountant, don't make one of two sins: not asking for advice when you need it, and ignoring the advice you do receive. Consult with your accountant whenever there's a significant change in your life with tax or financial implications—such as your inheriting money, making a large investment, or receiving a payout from a pension plan.

For the names of local CPAs, call the Association of Certified Public Accountants in your state.

46

FINANCIAL PLANNERS

A good financial planner should be the quarterback of your retirement program, a generalist who knows a lot about investments, taxes, estate planning, etc.

And that's one problem with financial planners: Some of them take on too much. Few human beings are so gifted that they can function simultaneously as an accountant/insurance agent/investment adviser/lawyer/pension adviser. (The best planners tend to belong to firms that have other experts on tap.)

Another problem is that anyone can call himself or herself a financial planner. A few years ago, someone in Florida even signed up his dog as a member of a well-known financial-planning organization.

A third problem is that there are self-styled planners out there who just sell certain products—insurance, gold, load mutual funds, limited partnerships. Says Gary Pittsford, a planner in Indianapolis, "These people may give you bare bones general advice, charge you $500, sell you something that pays them a big commission—and then are gone forever."

But there *are* superb planners out there, and many of the very best are members of the Registry of Financial Planning Practitioners. You can get a list, free, by writing to the International Association for Financial Planning, 2 Concourse Parkway, Atlanta, GA 30328.

Many members of the Registry are also Certified Financial Planners, another impressive credential. For names of local planners, write to the Institute of Certified Financial Planners, 10065 East Harvard Avenue, Denver, CO 80231.

Accountants who have studied financial planning are another good choice. Write to the American Institute of Certified Public Accountants, Personal Financial Planning Division, 1211 Avenue of the Americas, New York, NY 10036.

For names of Chartered Financial Consultants, who are strong on insurance, write to the American Society of CLU and ChFC, 270 Bryn Mawr Avenue, Bryn Mawr, PA 19010.

Your best bet may be fee-only or fee-based planners, who do their utmost to avoid buying you any products that compensate them with commissions. (Check with the National Association of Fee-Only Personal Financial Advisors, 1130 Lake Cook Road, Suite 105, Buffalo Grove, IL 60089.) But fee-only planners aren't numerous, and many of the very best planners receive both fees and commissions. (Some subtract commissions from the fees they charge.) Still, do avoid planners if *most* of their income comes from commissions. "If 90% of a planner's income comes from insurance," says Eileen M. Sharkey, a former president of the Institute of CFPs, "it's not surprising that he or she thinks that insurance is the solution to most of your problems."

What if a planner works directly for a brokerage firm or insurance agency and sells the company's products? It's not an especially favorable sign. But Pittsford notes that these planners may be the only good ones whom middle-income people can afford. "Still," he adds, "they should be honest about telling you about the commissions they receive."

Also ask whether the planner specializes in dealing with clients approaching retirement; how long he or she has been in business (4 years is a minimum); and how many clients he or she has (50 to 70 approaches the maximum).

If any planners give investment advice, they must be registered with the Securities and Exchange Commission and must provide you with a document describing their background, whether they have ever been disciplined, and how they are paid.

Expect to pay $50 to $150 an hour or—for a full-fledged financial plan—1% or so of your total assets.

47

INSURANCE AGENTS

Insurance has become incredibly complicated, what with innovations like "universal variable" life insurance. Even choosing among simple life insurance policies has always called for a gift for mathematics. Just explaining a variable annuity to a timid soul requires a special talent. And then there's the arcana of estate planning and such complex concepts as QTIP trusts.

Understandably, not many insurance agents are up to it all. Your best bet is to choose not just any agent, but a Certified Financial Planner (CFP), a chartered financial consultant (ChFC), or at the very least a chartered life underwriter (CLU).

Life insurance agents don't enjoy the best of reputations, so it's surprising how many people lean on them for general financial advice. "There's only one in a hundred insurance agents you can trust your wallet with," says Charles E. Westcott, a lawyer in Boston. "Only one in a hundred regards himself as a professional—the needs of his client are more important than his own economic needs. And the first time an insurance agent says to you, 'I don't really think you need a $250,000 whole life policy,' you know you've found that one in a hundred."

Graydon Calder, a CFP in San Diego, complains that insurance agents tend to believe that insurance is the solution for all of life's problems, from "retirement planning to fixing the kitchen sink." (Calder, by the way, is a chartered life underwriter.)

Life insurance salespeople are usually either "captive" or exclusive agents (who work primarily for one company) or independent agents (who work for more than one company). But don't jump to the conclusion that independents are automatically better because they can offer you the least expensive policy. Independents may offer you the policy that gives them the biggest commissions. If you do use an independent agent, demand that he or she show you the differences in the costs of the policies he or she sells.

Look for an agent who has been in the business for four or five years, so he or she is likely to be around to give you follow-up service. Especially desirable are agents with lots of well-to-do clients; because of the high commissions they have received from big policies, they can probably afford to spend more time with you. Be skeptical of any agent who sells life, health, *and* property/casualty insurance: Few people are so wise as to have mastered all those different specialties.

If you're buying term insurance, do try one or more of the computerized services that identify low-cost policies. Discuss the report you receive with your agent. Among the companies: Insurance Information in Methuen, MA (1-800-472-5800); Insurance Quote in Chandler, AZ (1-800-972-1104); LifeQuote in Coral Gables, FL (1-800-843-1768); SelectQuote in San Francisco, CA (1-800-343-1985); and TermQuote in Dayton, OH (1-800-444-TERM).

One insurance company endorsed by bargain hunters is Jackson National Life in Lansing, MI.

48

LONG-TERM CARE INSURANCE

It's been estimated that someone between 75 and 84 has a 36% chance of requiring nursing home care, and remaining for one to five years. The average annual cost for nursing home care is $25,000 to $35,000.

Medicare, the government's health-care program for retirees, covers only a part of nursing home expenses. Medicaid covers more, but is only for poor people.

Long-term care insurance can keep people from exhausting their financial resources as they grow older, although people over 80 may not be able to get coverage.

Most policies pay a fixed dollar amount of benefits a day instead of paying benefits based on actual expenses.

Desirable features:

- A daily benefit equal to the current daily cost of care, with provision for increases because of inflation.
- A benefit period of four years of more.
- Guaranteed renewable for life.
- A waiting period suitable to the insured's circumstances.
- Policy issued by a financially sound insurance company.
- Coverage of Alzheimer's and other diseases.
- Benefits for any level of care—from skilled nursing care to home health care.
- No requirement of earlier hospital stay or skilled nursing care.

Check the provisions of various companies' policies.

QUESTIONS AND ANSWERS

How much money will I need to retire?

Sorry, there's no one answer for everyone. Are you still paying off a mortgage? Do you have a chronic illness? Do you vacation at a local beach or take round-the-world cruises? As a rough guide, you will need 60% to 70% of your yearly preretirement income.

When should I start saving for retirement?

Most people probably start in their forties and fifties or when they have paid their children's way through college. But the sooner you begin saving, the less money you'll need to save later on—because your early investments will have years longer to compound (tax-deferred, if you use retirement plans like IRAs).

How much should I save?

The rule of thumb is 10% of your income a year. You can't live on what you receive now? As the old saying goes, if you can't live on your income now, trying to live on 10% less won't make any difference.

What should I invest in?

Stocks, bonds, cash equivalents (Treasury bills, money market funds), and real estate. The percentages you put into each depend on your age, your overall prosperity, and your financial sophistication. The younger you are, the more you can tilt toward volatile investments—toward stocks. The older you are, the more you should tilt toward stable investments—toward bonds and cash equivalents. See Key 27, Asset Allocation.

Aren't stocks too risky?

Stocks are *volatile*—their prices rise and fall—which isn't quite the same as *risky*. And over the long run, stocks have proved a *far* better investment than bonds or cash equivalents.

The stock market tends to bob up and down over five-year periods. So, if you can wait several years before cashing in your holdings, by all means consider buying stocks.

Still, if you suspect you might commit the cardinal sin—sell your holdings just after the stock market has tumbled—postpone buying stocks until you learn better.

If you invest in a mutual fund of stocks, you'll get diversification and a professional money manager. Look for a fund with a good long-term record. If you know something about investing, do it on your own by buying shares of a no-load (no sales commission) fund.

How can I be sure that my investments will prosper?

Check that your portfolio is diversified—not just horizontally (stocks, bonds, and cash), but vertically (different types of stocks, bonds with different maturities and credit ratings).

Decide on how your portfolio should be allocated—divided among stocks, bonds, and cash—and keep your portfolio loosely within these guidelines.

Keep a cache of cash—six months' worth of income.

Don't rely on yourself and your stockbroker to manage your investments. Hire a mutual fund manager or a private money manager to decide which stocks to buy and sell. Or have your stockbroker buy mutual funds for you, after you check out the records of any funds he or she recommends.

Don't make major market-timing decisions—quickly going completely into or out of any investment area.

Practice dollar-cost averaging: Buy, or sell, any investments gradually, over a period of time.

Learn about investing. Read books and magazines on the subject.

How much should I count on Social Security?

Only about 20% to 40% of your retirement income should be supplied by Social Security—and the wealthier you are, the lower the percentage. That's why you should have other sources of income—retirement plans, personal savings, and a house with no, or a low, mortgage.

What should I do about pension-plan payouts?

You can invest them according to the asset-allocation model you have already been using. If you've been putting 50% in stocks and 50% in bonds, you might keep those percentages.

Should I plan on invading my principal in retirement?

Yes, but "slowly and carefully," to quote financial planner Paul Westbrook.

Should I plan on leaving my children and grandchildren anything?

That's up to you. Some rich people boast that they made their own fortunes, and they expect their children to emulate them. Others feel that they should leave their own descendants something along the lines of what their parents left *them*. My own view is that your children and grandchildren can't be too wealthy (though they can be too thin). Your children may become incapacitated; *their* children may become incapacitated. The expenses can be a nightmare. Leave your children whatever you can fairly comfortably spare. And think of their needs before you consider the needs of your alma mater or of other non-profit institutions. Charity does begin you-know-where.

Do fixed annuities make sense?

Yes, for two reasons: They protect you against dumb, or unlucky, investment decisions you might make. And they protect you against living so long that you use up all your assets.

What advisers should I call upon?

Accountants and *Certified* Financial Planners are probably your best bets. Better—as a rule—than insurance agents and stockbrokers. CFPs should be limited to fee-only or fee-based planners, and they should be licensed as registered investment advisers.

GLOSSARY

Adjusted gross income taxable income, as it appears on the last line of Form 1040; after deductions for contributions to tax-deferred retirement plans, alimony, business expenses, etc.

Annuity an insurance company product that guarantees you a regular income as long as you live, or for a certain period of time. While the annuity is building up value, taxes on the growth are tax deferred. An immediate annuity begins paying you within a year; a deferred annuity pays you after a longer waiting period. A fixed annuity invests in a bond; a variable annuity invests in a vehicle whose value may fluctuate, like stocks.

Asset allocation how you invest the money in your portfolio among stocks, bonds, real estate, cash equivalents, etc.

Beta coefficient comparison of the volatility of an investment with the Standard & Poor's 500 stock index, which is given a beta of 1.

Blue chip Stock of an old, prosperous company, like Exxon.

Bond rating method of grading bonds by the issuer's ability to continue paying interest and to repay the lender's principal.

Capital gains/losses profits or losses on selling an asset, such as a stock, bond, or real estate.

Cash equivalents money you lend for a short time, as in money market funds, Treasury bills, and CDs that come due in a year or less.

Certificate of deposit investment purchased from a bank or brokerage house. Unlike bonds, CDs from a bank cannot easily be redeemed before they come due, but they are federally insured up to $100,000.

COLA (Cost of Living Adjustment) annual increase in Social Security benefits, if the cost of living rises enough.

Compounding Earning interest on your interest.

Conduit IRA Individual retirement account only for lump-sum distributions.

Default failure to pay interest on the loan, or to repay the principal when it comes due.

Defined-benefit plan pension plan with the focus on how much you will receive at retirement.

Defined-contribution plan pension plan that focuses on how much you or your employer contribute every year.

Deflation economic period when prices fall.

Discount product that sells for less than its face value. A discount bond trades for less than what the lender will pay you when the bond comes due.

Discretionary account arrangement in which a stockbroker or money manager trades for you without getting your approval first.

Diversification spreading out investments, horizontally (stocks, bonds, real estate) or vertically (a variety of stocks).

Dollar-cost averaging investing in an asset gradually, over the years, in relatively small, equal amounts of money.

Employee Stock Ownership Plan (ESOP) form of company-sponsored savings plan where employees can obtain the stock of their employer.

Estate all your assets.

Estate planning arranging for your assets to go to your heirs as you designate, with a minimum amount of federal and state taxes.

Face value What an investment will be worth when it comes due, or what a life insurance policy will pay in the event of a death.

Financial planners advisers who supervise all of their clients' financial affairs. The most common credential: CFP, Certified Financial Planner.

Fixed-income investments financial instruments, like bonds and certificates of deposit, that promise you regular payments during their term.

401(k) plans salary-reduction retirement plan offered by many large employers. Money taken out of your salary is not taxed; the employer may match part of your contribution.

Forward-averaging method of reducing the tax on assets taken out of certain retirement plans, like Keoghs and 401(k)s. The money will be taxed as if it had been withdrawn over five or ten years.

Hard assets gold, silver, other precious metals, real estate, antiques and collectibles, and so forth. Financial assets, like stocks and bonds, are "soft" assets.

Individual retirement account tax-deferred retirement plan available to workers who are not covered by company pension plans, or whose income is limited.

Inflation economic period when prices rise.

Joint and survivor annuity investment that guarantees income to two or more people, usually a husband and wife.

Junk bonds bonds that get low ratings because of uncertainty surrounding their issuers' financial stability. Also called high-yield bonds.

Keogh (HR-10) plans tax-deferred retirement plans for the self-employed.

Limited partnership vehicle for investing in which the investor is a direct owner but has no responsibility for management or liability for the partnership's debts beyond his or her initial investment. The general partner manages the investment.

Liquidity how readily an investment can be converted into cash.

Load sales charge on a mutual fund.

Lump-sum distribution payment an employer makes on the balance due an employee from a pension or profit-sharing plan.

Maturity date that borrowed money must be paid back.

Money market deposit account investment vehicle offered by banks; permits investors to put their money into short-term debt; usually pays less than money market funds and restricts withdrawals to two or three a month; federally insured.

Money market fund investment vehicle, offered by mutual funds and brokerage houses, that permits investors to put their money into high-paying, short-term debt. Unlike money market deposit accounts, these funds are usually not insured.

Municipal bond bond issued by a city, state, county, or public agency, the interest from which is typically not taxed by the government.

Payouts distributions from a company's pension or profit-sharing plan.

Portfolio all the assets someone owns; sometimes divided into retirement and personal portfolios.

Premium extra amount someone pays to buy something. A bond that is paying an unusually high interest rate may sell for more than its face value—at a premium.

Primary insurance amount the largest benefit a worker can receive from Social Security upon retirement.

Probate court procedure establishing the validity of a will and supervising the distribution of the estate's assets.

Profit-sharing plans savings plans, offered by employers, in which the amount of money given to employees may vary from year to year, and usually accumulates without being taxed.

Qualified plan a pension plan that meets IRS requirements, so the payments can be tax-deductible or tax free.

Real estate investment trusts publicly held companies that invest in various types of real estate, including mortgage debt.

Reverse annuity mortgage arrangement whereby an older homeowner receives regular payments from, say, a bank, in return for the bank's eventually having rights to the home.

Risk possibility that investors will lose all or part of their money, or will not receive enough compensation compared to what they could have earned safely elsewhere, or that the compensation will not match the rate of inflation.

Rollover distribution from a retirement plan that you reinvest in another retirement plan within 60 days of your receiving the money, so as to avoid a tax penalty.

Securities stocks, bonds, and similar investments.

Simplified employee pensions (SEPs)   tax-deferred retirement plans for the self-employed.

Single premium annuity annuity that someone buys with a single large payment.

Spread difference between the asking price and the bid price for an investment, like a bond.

Standard deviation number representing the volatility of an investment over a period of time. Used to measure the investment's riskiness.

Standard & Poor's 500 Stock Index proxy for the stock market as a whole. Both the S&P 500 and the Dow Jones Industrial average (of 30 stocks) emphasize big-company stocks.

Tax shelters investment vehicles that either defer federal taxation, like Keogh retirement plans, or escape it altogether, like the interest from municipal bonds.

Total return how much your original investment grows or shrinks—taking into consideration both the amount invested and the accumulated interest and dividends.

Treasury obligations fixed-income investments available from the U.S. Department of the Treasury. Bills are short-term (with maturities up to one year); notes are intermediate-term (two to ten years); bonds are long-term (ten to 30 years). The longer the term, typically, the higher the interest rate.

Trust   legal device created by the owner of assets to administer and distribute the assets—on behalf of the owner or of other people, such as heirs.

12b-1 fees fees that a mutual fund is permitted to take out of assets to pay for marketing costs.

Unified tax credit amount of money that you have available that escapes estate taxes. The word "unified" applies to federal estate taxes and gift taxes.

Unit investment trust type of mutual fund, typically a diversified portfolio of bonds, in which the bonds are bought and then held to maturity. Shareholders receive interest regularly, and—when the bonds in the trust mature—receive their principal.

Universal life insurance form of life insurance in which the policy holder can vary payments to both insurance coverage and cash buildup. Usually provides a competitive interest rate.

Vesting employee's right to pension money contributed by the employer, typically after a period of years.

Will legal document that expresses a person's wishes regarding the disposition of his or her estate.

Yield how much an investment regularly earns every year. A stock that sells at $100 a share and pays a $2 dividend four times a year has a yield of 8% ($8/$100 = 0.08).

Yield to maturity yield from a bond when you consider both the current yield and the difference between the bond's price now and the payment you will receive when the bond comes due.

Zero-coupon bond a bond—corporate, Treasury, or municipal—in which the yearly interest payments are added to the principal, and you receive one large sum at maturity. The "phantom" payments will be taxable every year, except in the case of municipals.

APPENDIX

Good Fixed-Income Funds

These no-sales-charge funds have good long-term records, according to the publication *Morningstar Mutual Funds.* Someone who needs income might invest in a few different types of fixed-income funds, recognizing that high-yield or "junk" bonds can be risky. T. Rowe Price Spectrum Income is composed mostly of other T. Rowe Price fixed-income funds, and this one investment provides broad diversification.

Corporate Bonds

Fund	Minimum	800 Number
Loomis Sayles Bond	$2,500	633-3330
Vanguard Fixed-Income Corporate	$3,000	662-7447
Strong Advantage	$1,000	368-1030
Portico Bond Index	$1,000	228-1024
Harbor Bond	$2,000	422-1050

Government Bonds

Fund	Minimum	800 Number
Strong Government Securities	$1,000	368-1030
Dreyfus Short-Intermediate	$2,500	645-6561
Vanguard Fixed-Income Short-Term Federal	$3,000	662-7447
Fidelity Spartan Limited Maturity Government	$10,000	544-8888
Benham GNMA Income	$1,000	331-8331

Specialty Bonds

Fund	Minimum	800 Number
Fidelity Spartan High-Income ("junk")	$1,000	544-8888
Fidelity Convertible Securities	$2,500	544-8888
Scudder International Bond	$1,000	225-2470
T. Rowe Price Spectrum Income	$2,500	638-5660
Northeast Investors ("junk")	$1,000	225-6704

References

For additional information on investment strategies before retirement, please see the following Barron's titles:

Keys to Choosing a Financial Specialist
Keys to Conservative Investments
Keys to Improving Your Return on Investments (ROI)
Keys to Investing in Common Stocks, 2nd ed.
Keys to Investing in Corporate Bonds
Keys to Investing in Government Securities, 2nd ed.
Keys to Investing in International Stocks
Keys to Investing in Mutual Funds, 2nd ed.
Keys to Investing in Options and Futures
Keys to Investing in Real Estate, 2nd ed.
Keys to Investing in Your 401(k)
Keys to Personal Financial Planning, 2nd ed.
Keys to Risks and Rewards of Penny Stocks
Keys to Understanding the Financial News, 2nd ed.
Keys to Understanding Securities

INDEX

142

NOTES

NOTES

NOTES

BARRON'S BUSINESS KEYS Each "key" explains approximately 50 concepts and provides a glossary and index. Each book: Paperback, 160 pp., 4 3/16" x 7", $4.95, Can. $6.50. ISBN Prefix: 0-8120.

Keys for Women Starting or Owning a Business (4609-9)
Keys to Avoiding Probate and Reducing Estate Taxes (4668-4)
Keys to Business and Personal Financial Statements (4622-6)
Keys to Buying a Foreclosed Home (4765-6)
Keys to Buying a Franchise (4484-3)
Keys to Buying and Owning a Home (4251-4)
Keys to Buying and Selling a Business (4430-4)
Keys to Choosing a Financial Specialist (4545-9)
Keys to Conservative Investments (4762-1)
Keys to Estate Planning and Trusts, 2nd Edition (1710-2)
Keys to Financing a College Education, 2nd Edition (1634-3)
Keys to Improving Your Return on Investments (ROI) (4641-2)
Keys to Incorporating (3973-4)
Keys to Investing in Common Stocks (4291-3)
Keys to Investing in Corporate Bonds (4386-3)
Keys to Investing in Government Securities (4485-1)
Keys to Investing in International Stocks (4759-1)
Keys to Investing in Mutual Funds, 2nd Edition (4920-9)
Keys to Investing in Options and Futures (9005-5)
Keys to Investing in Real Estate, 2nd Edition (1435-9)
Keys to Investing in Your 401(K) (1873-7)
Keys to Managing Your Cash Flow (4755-9)
Keys to Mortgage Financing and Refinancing, 2nd Edition (1436-7)
Keys to Personal Financial Planning, 2nd Edition (1919-9)
Keys to Personal Insurance (4922-5)
Keys to Purchasing a Condo or a Co-op (4218-2)
Keys to Reading an Annual Report (9240-6)
Keys to Retirement Planning (9013-6)
Keys to Risks and Rewards of Penny Stocks (4300-6)
Keys to Saving Money on Income Taxes (4467-3)
Keys to Starting a Small Business (4487-8)
Keys to Surviving a Tax Audit (4513-0)
Keys to Understanding Bankruptcy, 2nd Edition (1817-6)
Keys to Understanding the Financial News, 2nd Edition (1694-7)
Keys to Understanding Securities (4229-8)
Keys to Women's Basic Professional Needs (4608-0)

Available at bookstores, or by mail from Barron's. Enclose check or money order for full amount plus sales tax where applicable and 10% for postage & handling (minimum charge $3.75, Can. $4.00) Prices subject to change without notice.

Barron's Educational Series, Inc.
250 Wireless Blvd.
Hauppauge, NY 11788
In Canada: Georgetown Book Warehouse
34 Armstrong Ave., Georgetown, Ont. L7G 4R9   R 3/95

More selected BARRON'S titles:

ACCOUNTING HANDBOOK, 2nd EDITION, Joel G. Siegel and Jae K. Shim
Provides accounting rules, guidelines, formulas and techniques etc. to help
students and business professionals work out accounting problems.
Hardcover: $29.95, Canada $38.95/ISBN 6449-6, 864 pages

REAL ESTATE HANDBOOK, 3rd EDITION
Jack P. Freidman and Jack C. Harris
A dictionary/reference for everyone in real estate.
Defines over 1500 legal, financial, and architectural terms.
Hardcover, $29.95, Canada $39.95/ISBN 6330-9, 810 pages

**HOW TO PREPARE FOR THE REAL ESTATE LICENSING
EXAMINATIONS-SALESPERSON AND BROKER, 4th EDITION**
Bruce Lindeman and Jack P. Freidman
Reviews current exam topics and features updated model exams
and supplemental exams, all with explained answers.
Paperback, $11.95, Canada $15.95/ISBN 4355-3, 340 pages

**BARRON'S FINANCE AND INVESTMENT HANDBOOK,
4th EDITION,** John Downes and Jordan Goodman
This hard-working handbook of essential information defines more than 3000
key terms and explores 30 basic investment opportunities. The investment
information is thoroughly up-to-date. Hardcover $35.00, Canada $45.50/
ISBN 6465-8, approx. 1152 pages

FINANCIAL TABLES FOR MONEY MANAGEMENT
Stephen S. Solomon, Dr. Clifford Marshall, Martin Pepper,
Jack P. Freidman and Jack C. Harris
Pocket-sized handbooks of interest and investment rate tables used easily
by average investors and mortgage holders. Paperback
Real Estate Loans, 2nd Ed., $6.95, Canada $8.95/ISBN 1618-1, 336 pages
Mortgage Payments, 2nd Ed., $5.95, Canada $7.95/ISBN 1386-7, 304 pages
Bonds, 2nd, Ed., $5.95, Canada $7.50/ISBN 4995-0, 256 pages
Canadian Mortgage Payments, 2nd Ed., Canada $8.95/ISBN 1617-3, 336 pages
Adjustable Rate Mortgages, 2nd Ed., $6.95, Canada $8.50/ISBN 1529-0, 288 pages

All prices are in U.S. and Canadian dollars and subject to change without notice. At your
local bookseller, or order direct adding 10% postage (minimum charge $3.75, Canada $4.00),
N.Y. residents add sales tax.   ISBN PREFIX 0-8120

Barron's Educational Series, Inc.
250 Wireless Boulevard, Hauppauge, NY 11788
In Canada: Georgetown Book Warehouse
34 Armstrong Ave., Georgetown, Ontario L7G 4R9   R 3/95